"Practical Spirituality [...] road in our relationships [...] Authenticity, with integrity [...] actions, is the true path of [...] examples, Kathy Gottberg points the way for those wanting to take control of their own spiritual direction."
—Edgar Mitchell, Sc.D., Founder of Institute of Noetic Sciences

"Kathy Gottberg is a great guide for anyone embarking on a spiritual path. Her stories are invigorating, insightful, and full of light. Gottberg writes from her own deep wisdom, and weaves riches from the world's spiritual masters throughout her book. This is a book you can open anywhere and come upon an unexpectedly beautiful jewel that will lift your thinking and light your day. No matter where you are on your spiritual path, this book is one map you'll want to have in your pack."
—Jan Phillips, author of *Marry Your Muse, God Is at Eye Level,* and *Making Peace* >www.janphillips.com<

"Kathy Gottberg writes like an angel – clear and right to the point."
—Walter Starke, author of I*t's All God, The Golden Thread, Homesick For Heaven,* and other books.

"The charming and informative stories and illustrations make New Thought concepts accessible and understandable to any reader. Those new to the New Thought philosophy will have the opportunity to explore basic practical spirituality, while experienced "old timers" are treated to a fresh approach to New Thought universal concepts. I particularly enjoyed the tips and suggestions offered to enhance our life experience."
—Angelo Pizelo, President of Emerson Institute

"*The Findhorn Book of Practical Spirituality* is well written, beautifully simple, and an entertaining guide to the perennial philosophy and Science of Mind."
—Chris Powell, RN. Ph.D.

"A readable, personable, and understandable walk through practical spirituality. This is an *easy-to-assimilate* slice of life and its principles and possibilities. Kathy has brought it to us in her own *easy to relate to*, warm and friendly style. A book filled with authenticity and charm."
—Rev. Deborah Gordon, Kelowna Center of Positive Living, Kelowna, British Columbia

"Kathy has woven a marvelous tapestry of sparkling stories, skillful questions, and simple suggestions for bringing spiritual principles into action in everyday life. A wonderful companion and guide on the path."
—Rudi Harst, Spiritual Director of the Celebration Circle in San Antonio, Texas and author of *Hurry Slowly*

"Kathy Gottberg's *Practical Spirituality*, with its clear, sometimes light and humorous explanation of how New Thought works, is a great gift to seekers of workable spirituality. Her meaningful personal examples add authenticity and rich color to her writings. A true find for beginners on the path, as well as for those who search for deeper understanding of Truth and its everyday use."
—Dr. Margaret Stevens, AGNT Advisor and author of *Families of the Jailed, a book of Hope*

"Kathy Gottberg has succeeded in breaking out the essential questions and issues in easily understood terms. I think *Practical Spirituality* will be a welcome addition to any beginning, serious student of metaphysical truth."
—Rev. Toni Hegge, Centre of Positive Living, Calgary, Alberta, Canada

"We live in an unprecedented time of knowledge and information. The brightest thinkers of our time may be accessed by all, not just the privileged few. However, integrating this wisdom into the average life of our time is what *Practical Spirituality* shares within its pages. It is one thing to read knowledge, but quite another to be it."
—Sharon Ince, Doctor of Divinity

THE
FINDHORN
BOOK OF

Practical Spirituality

A Down-to-Earth Guide to a Miraculous Life

by

Kathy Gottberg

First published by Findhorn Press 2003

ISBN 1 84409 007 8

British Library Cataloguing-in-Publication Data.
A catalogue record for this book is available from
the British Library.

Edited by Shari Mueller
Cover and internal book design by Thierry Bogliolo

Printed and bound by WS Bookwell, Finland

Published by
Findhorn Press
305a The Park, Findhorn
Forres IV36 3TE
Scotland, UK

tel 01309 690582
fax 01309 690036
e-mail: info@findhornpress.com

findhornpress.com

TABLE OF CONTENTS

ACKNOWLEDGEMENTS

I am extraordinarily grateful to wake up each morning to a life where I'm allowed to playfully and creatively participate in All That Is. I am profoundly thankful for my relationship with Thom, my partner, lover, and best friend. May the next 25 years be as awesome as the first! I am grateful for fantastic friends and family members, living on a beautiful section of Mother Earth, vibrant health, financial wellbeing, numerous freedoms and a joyful and optimistic heart. Deep appreciation goes to my support buddies: Donna Hathaway, Jamie O'Neil, Brenda Gunderson, Ernesto Lopez, Ann Thill and, of course, Thom. Your suggestions and words of encouragement were as valuable to me as your proofing. A special "Thank You," to Darren John Main, who is a great author, speaker and friend. His generosity initiated this book and it wouldn't exist without him. I am also grateful to the Palm Springs Center of Positive Living and everyone who has ever participated. The growth, challenge, love and friendship it gives, is the reason I show up. In the end, I thank All That Is for all that is. Namaste.

AUTHOR'S WEBSITE

www.kathygottberg.com

INTRODUCTION

A wise old woman lived in the little town of Broken Bow, Nebraska. Her crinkled and weathered face revealed eyes that appeared to see the answer to every question ever asked. A novelty among her neighbors, she mainly kept to herself unless approached by a townsperson in need of counsel.

One day the local children decided to trick the old woman. Seen only as eccentric and strange, they were completely unimpressed by her wisdom or reputation. One bold little boy came up with a plan where he would catch a small bird and hold it in his hands behind his back and say, "Old woman, is the bird in my hands alive or is it dead?" If the woman said the bird was alive, he intended to squeeze the life out of it; if the woman said it was dead, he would present the live bird, making her look foolish.

Later that week the children found the wise woman downtown and gathered around her in anticipation. She smiled softly at their eager faces and waited with patient interest until the little boy with the bird pushed his way up in front of her. "So wise woman, is the bird in my hand alive, or is it dead?"

The woman stood silent for a moment and took a long deep breath. Slowly, she bent down until she stood no higher than the boy, and gazed affectionately into his eyes, "The life you are holding," she said simply, "is in your hands."

As we stand at the beginning of the 21st Century, we face a future gleaming with tremendous possibility and opportunity. Like a pirate's treasure, the years ahead glitter with the untold promise of amazing technological advances, awe-inspiring creations, and depth defying information. At the same time, the future offers uncertainty, unpredictability, and unimaginable turmoil, much like the experience of free diving from a cliff without a parachute. While our future may indeed lie in our own hands, what we do with it, how we hold it, remains a question of deep inquiry. After all, where does a person go to find a wise woman, when few of us live in Nebraska, and when most of the old women we know prefer to live in senior retirement communities?

One of the best answers exists in the realm of practical spirituality. Practical spirituality is not a religion. It works regardless of your faith, or where or how you were raised. Practical spirituality takes the wisdom and universal truths running through all religions and philosophies, and distills and refines those elements with the intention of creating a life filled with happiness, meaning, and miracles. In other words, practical spirituality repeatedly demonstrates, in a down-to-earth manner, that the life you are holding is in your hands. Once realized, you can then choose what to do about it.

WhAT DOES PRACTICAL SPIRITUALITY LOOK LIKE?

Before we go further, it is necessary to define practical spirituality in a way that not only makes sense, but is also easy to recognize. Most of us carry around a vague interpretation of what we think spiritual means, but that definition has come under great scrutiny in the last couple of decades. Who really is spiritual when repeated scandals concerning money, sexual conduct, and simple human compassion scream from the front pages of our daily newspapers? Perhaps it is time for a new vision of a spiritual life?

Until recently, an otherworldly, out-of-reach, select group of humans, with a direct and exclusionary access to the Divine controlled our vision of

God and religion. Could that be part of the problem? As long as we see separation between average individuals, and those glorified as our spiritual leaders, we never expect much of ourselves. I heard it said in Native American tribal wisdom, "If you are riding a dead horse, the best strategy is to dismount." I say, "If the horse is clearly aged and frail, why wait?"

Obviously, it is time for a change, but how do we start defining this new down-to-earth spiritual person? One way is to list the qualities found in people we universally admire and respect for their spiritual actions. Below are ten characteristics that exist regardless of religion or ethnicity. Do you recognize any of the following in yourself?

AUTHENTICITY

An authentic person speaks the truth not because she never wants to lie, but because she believes there is no compelling reason to avoid it. Many of us don't tell the truth because we think others don't want to hear it, or because we believe that we will lose the love and acceptance of the person we are talking to if we told them what we really thought. The authentic person never allows her fear to compromise her essential nature.

Of course, authenticity is more than just telling the truth. Authentic people are true to themselves first. They believe that their life has a purpose, and when confronted by choices, they choose the path that corresponds most closely to that purpose. They ignore the pull of guilt, shame, or conditioning that asks them to toe the line or conform, and respond from their spiritual nature rather than their human nature. An authentic person acts from the inside out, rather than the outside in.

Authenticity also requires us to "walk our talk." This characteristic has captured our attention lately, because in the past we repeatedly denied and overlooked many discrepancies from our leaders in the name of conformity. However, in the 21st Century few people can hide their actions for long. Moreover, because they cannot hide, neither can we. When we overlook people's inconsistencies and incongruities, we endorse the behavior and define ourselves at the same time. Authenticity demands that we do what we say, and say what we do, to a higher and more consistent standard.

WHOLENESS

The word holy comes from the root word for whole. Wholeness is essential for practical spirituality because it allows a person to be in the world, and at the same time, unified with the dimensions beyond it. Up until recently, most people who devoted their lives to God were required to renounce life and stand apart. Perhaps that is why it is tempting to define spiritual people by their withdrawal rather than their participation in life.

Practical spirituality opens the door and allows us to connect to everything that exists, both the things of the world and the things of the spirit. There is no denying the pleasures of the body—everything from roller coasters to hot fudge sundaes to physical intimacy—each nesting in the wholeness of God, as much as the pleasures of the spirit, the bliss of Oneness, or the awe of unconditional love.

Both the words "holy" and "sacred" are often thought to mean something divorced from our ordinary experience. Yet, if everything is God, if everything exists within Universal Oneness, then everything is sacred and holy. Living in the paradox of heaven on earth is the realm of practical spirituality.

AWAKE AND AWARE

The new spiritual person is awake and aware most of the time. In other words, he is present in each moment, and when he is with you, you know it. His attention and focus allows him to be master of most of his endeavors, everything from making a living, to becoming closer to God. Even in those areas where his habits are less than the most desirable, he is fully conscious of the choices he is making and chooses either to continue, stop, or change courses.

Most of us are locked into habits we don't remember adopting. The choices we make are often unconscious, and even in the midst of them we forget we had a choice to begin with. As we awaken gradually to our true spiritual nature, we catch ourselves in all sorts of actions that don't serve our highest purpose. Thankfully, that catching gets easier and happens more quickly when we make the effort to stay awake.

HARMONIOUS

The person who practices spirituality in a practical way keeps her heart open and active and, at the same time, lives in an experience of harmony with the Universe. This is not the same as withdrawal or passivity, although many in the past have done that and called it spiritual. A harmonious person avoids reacting to the external feedback going on around her. In tune with that still, small voice within, she sees the circumstances of her life, and the lives of those around her, as a symphony, never losing sight of the essential, underlying melody of Spirit.

This is like a man who discovered a bear was chasing him. The man ran in the opposite direction as fast as he could until he came to a cliff. Unable to stop, he fell over the side. As he tumbled down the edge, he grabbed hold of a vine and clung with all his might. Above, he saw the bear reaching over the edge with huge swipes of his massive paw. There was no going back. Below him sat sharp jagged rocks. There was no going down.

Just then, he glanced at the vines holding him against the ledge, and saw two mice chewing on the roots and very nearly cutting through. Faced with the inevitable moment, his eyes locked on the scruffy vine where one plump red strawberry grew within his reach. Plucking it, he put it into his mouth. His only response was, "Ah...delicious."

EQUIVALENCE

While equivalence might not be a word you use frequently, you recognize the action when you see it. In the presence of an individual who practices practical spirituality, everyone feels respected and valued. There is no sense of superiority, authority, or ego. He doesn't bore you with everything he thinks he knows, but rather spends time asking you about you. There is no effort to fix, control, manipulate, or change you in any way. What unusual behavior!

One thing that you will notice is that a person practicing spirituality includes everyone, and excludes no one. She doesn't question whether women are equal to men, or whether there are differences between race, sexuality, or religion. She radiates a connection to all people, as well as a unity with all of life. If everything is God, how could one thing or one person be any better than another?

LIGHTHEARTED AND OPTIMISTIC

In the past, a spiritual person was expected to be serious, somber, and radiate the suffering of humanity. Then came the Dalai Lama. We finally have a spectacular example of how to live a life of joy without being so serious! Certainly, the Dalai Lama has faced numerous challenges, like the loss of his country, the death of hundreds of his friends, and the continual alienation of his heritage. Yet, in every conversation, he is filled with light-heartedness, joy, and optimism.

I don't know about you, but I think we have seen enough examples of those who demonstrate a mournful approach to God. If the Divine is truly all-powerful, all knowing, and everywhere present, then why should we be so sad? Sadness and fear exist in a people who think they are separate and cut off from the infinite source and goodness of the Universe. Don't you think that anyone who knew and lived a deep connection to Spirit would look like he just won the biggest lottery of all time? How could anyone deeply connected to the soul of the Universe forget that a miracle is possible in every moment?

ALWAYS GROWING AND EVOLVING

Most of us detest not knowing the correct answer to something. We will skirt around any issue, or even lie, rather than just admit, "I don't know." We have demanded a definitive answer to everything, and carried that to the extreme with our political leaders, healthcare professionals, and religious authorities. Then, if they act vulnerable or ignorant, we condemn them with the worst kind of criticism. Maybe it is time to recognize that it is impossible to know everything in the first place, and even then, things can change. That includes us, that includes Life, and that includes Spirit. Practical spirituality defines God as an ever-expanding mystery.

Yet, many of us, in our need to make God something safe and under-standable, lock It in a box and try to make It an absolute. Then, only those who hold a key to that special box are considered worthy of enlightenment. However, is it possible that God is so magnificent, so awesome, so myste-rious, so constantly unfolding that the only way to know Spirit is to grow, evolve, and unfold, in the same way? The new model of a spiritual person is one who constantly reaches, grows, plays, and explores. Ultimately, God as an emergent adventure sounds much more glorious than God as a rigid absolute.

ACCOUNTABLE

This quality is not an attempt to make you or me responsible for the entire Universe. Instead, this is recognition that a person who practices practical spirituality is 100% accountable for himself, his life, and his reaction in every moment.

This also goes beyond any idea that you created the bad or tragic events that happened to you or your loved ones. You aren't that powerful. What you do have is the ability and the consciousness to co-create the course and direction of everything that happens from now forward. Even though you don't make things happen on your own, you are connected, and to some extent, a part of everything going on around you.

Blaming God or other people for what occurs is useless. A person on the new spiritual path sees the wholeness, the connection, and her participation. While it may be difficult to look into every circumstance and see God, it is only a clouded vision that blurs the view.

The best news about accountability is that it gives us unlimited options. Instead of feeling victimized and put upon by circumstances or others, we can choose to learn from any experience. We can also make changes and adjustments so that the next time we find ourselves facing the same situation, it has a different outcome. Accountability helps us reclaim our power as co-creators of Life.

GENEROSITY AND SERVICE

Mother Teresa devoted her entire life to spiritual service. She referred to it as serving her "Beloved." Comparing our lives to hers can be very intimidating. Nevertheless, true service doesn't need to be grand to be important. Mostly it just means that we act selflessly in kindness and compassion to all that we call our Beloved, or Spirit.

It might seem that it takes a lot of time to be of service but the funny thing is that those in service are often those who have more than the usual amount of distractions. It doesn't take time, it take prioritizing. A person choosing to practice spirituality in a practical way knows that only those things freely shared are truly owned. Therefore, he focuses on giving, rather than getting.

A kind act, or offering appreciation to the person behind the checkout counter, can be a true act of service. Helping those in need without the slightest expectation of return, is an act of love. Providing vision and inspiration to anyone who lacks hope is an act of kindness. Recognizing that what we do for others, we do for ourselves, is a holy practice.

FEARLESSNESS

Face it; it takes courage to live as a practical spiritual person in our world. It is far easier to keep attending the church of our childhood and keep our mouth shut, or stop going altogether. In Australia, they call it the "tall poppy syndrome." When poppies grow they tend to all grow to the same height. However, now and then one grows higher than the rest and that poppy is usually picked first, or cut down before any of the others. Parents in Australia warn their children not to be the tall poppy, and we caution each other about the same thing in many ways.

We have all heard stories of what happens to people when they stand out and make a difference. After all, consider the lives of Jesus, Gandhi, or Martin Luther King, Jr. While most of us deny that we are afraid to be different, our lives are amazingly similar. Many settle for lives of quiet desperation, striving as Will Rogers said, "to go to jobs we hate, to make money to buy things we don't need, to impress people we don't even like." The problem with that is, as Lily Tomlin says, "even if you win at the rat race, you're still a rat."

In a world where everything is sacred and holy, every one of us is important. That means you, me, and the other 6.5 billion people on the planet. While we are obviously different and unique expressions of the Universal Life Force, we have a valuable part to play in our world. Moreover, chances are if we don't perform our role, it won't happen. Having the courage and the willingness to show up, take action, and give of ourselves, even if we are afraid, even if there are consequences, is an act of practical spirituality.

Helen Keller, who was deaf and blind, said, "Security is mostly a superstition. It does not exist in nature, nor do the children of men as a whole experience it. Avoiding danger is no safer in the end than outright exposure. Life is either a daring adventure or nothing. To keep our faces toward change and behave like free spirits in the presence of fate is strength undefeatable."

If you have been waiting for someone out there to come and save you or the world, you just might be the person you are waiting for.

MY PATH

I would like to say I found practical spirituality, but truthfully, it found me. Nearly two decades ago I started on a spiritual path much different from the one of my youth. I wasn't particularly dissatisfied with the church where I grew up; I just gradually discovered it had little or no relevance in my everyday life. I needed and wanted something, but I knew intuitively it didn't exist in my past.

My search focused on the study of New Thought. New Thought is an American religion developed during the last 100 or so years. It utilizes the universal principles found in most of the world's major religions, and synthesizes the best of their teachings and concepts, especially those suited to the western mind. It fit me, and answered the questions in my heart. Although I continue to evolve from what I originally studied, it remains as my primary foundation.

My biggest spiritual leap came when I realized that no matter how much I studied, or how much the interpretations of New Thought resonated within my heart, something was lacking. The missing element was the practical application of the ideas in my head. Regardless of how wonderful spiritual concepts are, only when we are able to internalize them, and then actualize them, do we become the message we are attempting to convey.

There is a story about a mother who asked Mahatma Gandhi to tell her son not to eat sugar. After taking her son to the doctor and learning that he was diabetic, the mother did everything she could to stop her son from eating sweets. The child however, continued to sneak candy whenever possible. As a last resort, she sought out the power and advice of India's most revered person, Gandhi.

After waiting for hours, the woman and her son finally stood before the man. She said, "Please tell my son to stop eating sugar, it's very bad for him."

Instead of saying anything to the boy, Gandhi instead asked the woman to return in three weeks. Confused but compliant, the woman nodded and left with her son.

Three weeks later, again after a long, tiring wait, the woman and her son stood before Gandhi. Once again she asked, "Please sir, would you tell my son to stop eating sugar?"

Immediately Gandhi turned to the boy and said, "Boy, you must not eat sugar."

The mother, frustrated by the heat and the long wait, asked Gandhi, "But why didn't you just say that three weeks ago?"

Gandhi looked at the mother and replied, "Because three weeks ago I was still eating sugar myself."

Throughout his life, Gandhi strove to be the message, rather than to teach a message. Although unusual, this approach is what practical spirituality is all about. While it is relatively easy to learn the principles of any of the world's major religions and to recite them at will, it is much more difficult to stop eating sugar before we have the audacity to tell others to do so. Practical spirituality demands it.

In my own life, I discovered that even if the lessons and the ideas I was learning sounded empowering and life affirming, the only way they had any meaning was to live them on a regular basis. I confess I frequently fall short, yet the striving continually raises me higher than I ever would have gone otherwise. That is the power of practical spirituality.

Eight years ago, my husband Thom and I, founded a spiritual community in our city in an attempt to create a model of what churches may become in the 21st Century. Operating without a guide or structure, we wanted to see if it was possible. A calling within us wanted to discover if the most current spiritual and philosophical concepts could hold up in a new environment of respect, love, and tolerance for all spiritual paths. We also wanted to be part of an organization beyond hierarchy, or beyond the standard authoritarian leadership models that dominate most church communities. Our vision was a practical, democratic, all volunteer, spiritual organization that put into practice all the ideas and inspiration it talked about, and did it in an atmosphere of freedom, love, respect, and possibility.

The action of co-creating an organization with others pushed us into practicing our spirituality on a level far beyond that of mere student. We were no longer tourists to a new realm of being; we were settlers in a new landscape of spiritual potential. Naturally, there were plenty of people to tell us it wouldn't work. Others said, "No one will financially support a group that doesn't have a minister or one leader." To the contrary, from day one, donations have kept us financially successful and self-sufficient. Others told us that we couldn't maintain our own personal businesses and lives, and at the same time participate fully in an on-going spiritual community. Again to the contrary, our personal finances grow stronger every year, and our relationship has deepened and matured in all ways. Others doubted our commitment and questioned our ability to continue. Yet, our lives have been so miraculously rewarded as a direct result of our willingness to carry on, that we'd be crazy to stop showing up now.

While I am not suggesting you go out and start your own spiritual community, I would like this book to serve as an invitation. I invite you to see if examples from my life, and the lives of many teachers I have met along the path, offer you the evidence you need to live a down-to-earth spiritual life. I guarantee that if you take the time to explore and put into practice some of the simple, profound, and practical steps I have discovered in the last fifteen years, you too will have a more happy, meaningful, and miraculous life. Remember, the life you are holding is in your hands.

Chapter One

WAKING UP!

Buzz-z-z-z-z-z-z! Have you heard it yet? Eventually, that wake-up alarm rings for everyone. Sometimes it hits us like a bolt of lightning, and other times it caresses us like the slow trickle of a stream on a late summer day. Frequently without warning, we wake up, open our eyes and discover nothing is the same. We feel different. We are different. Depending upon your perspective, and your personality, that change is either exhilarating, painful, or somewhere in between.

Movies, novels and parables throughout history illuminate the path. Some offer warnings, while others entice us with possibilities or adventure. It is not amazing that we hear the call, what appears most unusual is that it happens so frequently and some still don't notice. Apparently, the wake up alarm buzzes for everyone, yet many hit the snooze button and drift back to sleep.

The Zen Buddhist tradition explains this by saying that when a person is ready, a leaf can brush past them and they will be enlightened. If not, a tree can land squarely on their head and there will be no perceivable difference. Experiences themselves appear as varied as each individual. However, one thing that does seem to be consistent is that when you ignore the call, it tends to become increasingly insistent as it clamors for your attention.

I began to wake up in my late thirties. About that time, a slight, but gnawing, dissatisfaction began growing within both Thom and me. Our early dream of being millionaires by age 40 seemed improbable and vaguely unmotivating. Like many others our age, we were starting to look at one another after ten plus years of marriage with the question, "Is this all there is?"

Our spark to awaken was a visit to the local bookstore and Thom's impulse to select a small metaphysical book from the self-help area. The primary message we extracted from that little book was a reminder that life was both mysterious and miraculous. It had nothing to do with religion, and everything to do with what it called "spirituality." Clearly, our lives had more purpose and meaning than how much money we made, what kind of job we had, where we lived, or what kind of car we drove. It stripped away the superficiality of life as we had been living, and put us in touch with thousands of other people on a similar path who were aware of an undeniable connection to the phenomenon of life. It confirmed that we, too, could live happy and extraordinary lives just by hearing the call of our soul.

We were not alone. Not only were there millions of other people who embraced these amazing concepts, there were also many groups, organizations, and even churches on this path. A quick look through the phone book confirmed it. Listed under New Thought and Interdenominational categories were groups like Unity, Religious Science, and more with names like "Positive Living" and "Enrichment Center."

It took several tries. We attended a handful of the organizations we found listed, and several others we discovered by keeping our eyes open. The saying, "that which you are seeking is seeking you," was evident. One Sunday morning we attended a New Thought church with a message unlike any from our childhood. Noticeably absent were messages of guilt, control, or pessimism. The group itself radiated a sense of optimism, peace and acceptance. Finally, we felt we found a place where we could explore and learn about a loving and benevolent world to which we were intimately linked. Gradually, and I do mean gradually, that world became our world too.

On the other hand, my friend Georgia's wake up call was dramatically different. Living within a traditional religious background for most of her childhood and early adult life, Georgia did it all, everything from attending church seven days a week, to naming her three children with names from the Bible. Eventually however the dogma, control and stifling repression she found within those religions repelled her to the point where she walked away from everything, her first husband included.

Believing that freedom must be an attribute of the spirituality she craved, Georgia began to live and raise her children from that principle. This appeared to work, until her eldest son stood at the edge of that freedom, high on drugs and self-destruction, and challenged it all.

Filled with guilt that her approach to spirituality was flawed and that she was responsible for the danger her son faced, Georgia spent an agonizing three days outside on her patio without food or sleep. There she questioned everything she knew about God and how it affected her life. Finally, in a moment of complete frustration and surrender, transformation happened.

In a flash, she was filled with a sense that the only thing she could or should do, was to love. She knew then that love was the freedom she craved and that love itself made all things whole. Love integrated the paradox she had always resisted between the rules and the freedom she saw everywhere around her. Suddenly, in her exhilarated state, she knew she was connected to every other person and to all life. Love was all that was necessary.

Eventually Georgia discovered that her exalted state is sometimes called a cosmic consciousness experience. That intense joy, and its accompanying transformation, turned her entire life around and remains with her today. She now sees the world as whole and integrated, and senses an ever-unfolding depth behind things that before only appeared superficial. With her new set of priorities, Georgia abandoned most of the excess in her life, changed many of her friends and acquaintances, and committed herself to social service whenever possible. Beyond that, she began to read hundreds of books and listen to thousands of tapes, all of which expanded her mind and heart. Most importantly, Georgia began to live the message of love that she learned that day on her porch. Miraculously, within hours of her experience, her son entered a rehabilitation program and since then has chosen to avoid all aspects of a destructive path.

While we may be tempted to think of Georgia's experience as a miracle, the process of change and transformation is actually very natural. The new science of nonlinear dynamics and Chaos Theory has a name for the point of waking up called bifurcation. Bifurcation is the "fork in the road," that we, and every element of nature, continually face as we grow, evolve and change. Like a fragile butterfly breaking out of a decayed cocoon, that sometimes disorienting process of letting go of the old and embracing the new is the bifurcation point of waking up.

It is good to remember we have a choice in the process. Something I read long ago maintained that we tend to make changes and grow in one of two ways. The first way, and obviously the easiest, is through divine inspiration. You could call this the guidance of your highest self. Unfortunately, on more than one occasion, many of us choose the second, the path of pain and suffering. As a participant within a spiritual community, I have seen others take both paths, and have taken both as well. Remember, we do not just choose once and that is it. Life is a continual process of evolution prompted by either inspiration or pain, forcing us beyond what is comfortable and familiar.

During the last eight years, I have witnessed several people develop and transform in front of my eyes. Many people begin attending our group with the thought that they are doing so merely to make friends and to get to know other open minded people. Yet, as they attend, take classes and workshops, and become more involved throughout the years, their sense of Life and their connection to It, changes in a perceivable way. Most of them have not experienced a dramatic awakening, yet by listening to their intuition and following its guidance, they have answered the beckoning of their spirit.

On the other hand, I have observed people who attend our meetings occasionally and then disappear for months on end. When we see them again, it is usually because something soul shattering occurred and they are looking for answers. It may be that their significant other has abandoned them, they lost their job, or they are faced with some type of illness.

Whatever it is, their soul is screaming for their attention, and they suddenly remember that putting their Spirit first is a good idea. While getting involved with an organization may not be the answer, listening and following the prompting of one's soul is vital.

From my perspective, there is no right or wrong way to wake up, only the inevitable consequences to our actions or our non-actions. The choice is ours to ignore the inner urge, hit that snooze button, and live life bouncing back and forth between the external forces of fortune or disaster. Another choice is to avoid the call for a while until eventually, something happens that captures our attention. Finally, we can choose to follow the gentle urging of our soul and continually strive to go deeper and discover the treasure within.

A movie that came out several years ago entitled *Pleasantville* demonstrates this process in an interesting way. In the movie a young man and his sister were transported into an old television program, much like *Father Knows Best*, where things seemed so simple, uncomplicated and wholesome. Yet the experience of living within the black-and-white television program proved that conformity, consistency, and absence of freedom lacked soul or Life force. Even though things appeared perfect on the surface, the actual experience of it was fake and lifeless. As the characters gradually woke up to their creativity and individual self-expression, splashes of Technicolor filled the screen, until the entire movie was in vivid color. That story showed me that part of waking up might be an ongoing willingness and courage to sacrifice the known for the unknown.

Waking up offers an unexpected benefit that is overlooked frequently. Once we begin to follow the urgings of our soul and become more authentically ourselves, we in turn have more to offer other people and the world at large. An example of this comes from a man named Edgar Mitchell who was the sixth human to walk on the surface of our moon. This accomplishment makes him extraordinary, not to mention highly unusual. What makes him exceptional was what he did when he returned to Earth.

Back in 1971, after spending several intense days on the moon under extraordinary stress and hard physical labor, he found himself in a peaceful and relaxed state during the return trip. Floating in zero gravity, and with a hypnotic view of our planet beckoning him home, he experienced what he describes as an epiphany followed by intense exhilaration. From that moment, he was transformed.

What changed? As described in his book, *The Way of the Explorer: An Apollo Astronaut's Journey Through the Material and Mystical Worlds*, Mitchell explains it as a sense of deep and universal connectedness. As he gazed upon the planet, he both saw and felt how everything was unified, whole and perfect exactly as it was. That understanding included him and the planet, and extended out into the cosmos in every direction. It was not a religious experience, but rather an enlightening into the natural wholeness and evolution of All That Is. That profound knowledge and expanded view initiated his transformation.

Shortly thereafter Mitchell resigned from NASA and began an even more important mission—a journey of inner exploration. In 1972, he envisioned and then founded the Institute of Noetic Sciences (IONS), an organization that is dedicated to the study of consciousness and different states of knowing and becoming. During the last 30 years IONS has touched thousands of people around the world, serves as a leader in the consciousness movement, and continues to explore and validate the journey of inner space. Obviously Mitchell had many choices when he returned from our moon, yet there was something within him that, once awake, was not content to stop investigating the Mystery.

While few of us will ever journey to outer space, Edgar Mitchell is a good reminder that we can all take the fantastic voyage within. He also demonstrates how one person, listening to their call, can aid in the journey of thousands of others. If we are indeed an interconnected Whole, our awakening just might be the last piece of the puzzle necessary to complete a new era for us all.

What about people who hear no call whatsoever? Eventually it boils down to asking why we believe we were born and exist in the first place. If we think life is simply about acquiring possessions, conforming, playing it safe, and amusing ourselves until we die, then we probably resist the very idea of waking up. After all, who needs to see the world in a new way if we are perfectly happy and content with the way things are?

Waking up, then, is for those who can't go back to sleep. Or, as my friend Donna likes to say, "Once you know, you can't not know." The one-dimensional world that says "He who dies with the most toys wins," is a booby prize of cosmic proportion. While waking up does not guarantee an easier or more prosperous existence, or a world where nothing bad happens, it does pull us into the equation of a Universe filled with meaning and purpose. It strips away the shallow, and reveals what is true. Furthermore, if we intuitively acknowledge that the mystery of deep unity and self-expression are fundamental aspects of Life, then embracing the call of waking up is the most natural, joyful, and inspiring opportunity we ever face. Acknowledging that, allows us to know that wherever we are led, it is for our highest benefit.

One Hawaiian legend says that every baby born resembles a bowl filled with Light. Then, as the baby grows, she becomes indoctrinated and trained. She learns to conform and to do things so that others will love and accept her. This is like putting rocks in the bowl. These rocks are the rules and customs our society teaches us about how little girls and little boys should behave. As children grow into adults, their bowls become so heaped with rocks that only a tiny bit of their Light is visible. As we awaken, our purpose becomes to remove the rocks one-by-one and return to the Light that we are.

It is valuable to remember that we are not alone. At first Thom and I thought that our new way of thinking was so unusual, that few others would be willing to put aside the materialist dream in favor of an expanded consciousness. We were wrong. In the year 2000, a book entitled, *The Cultural Creatives—How 50 Million People Are Changing The World* by Paul H. Ray and Sherry Ruth Anderson explains how this emerging collection

of people is transforming the planet. While this group remains largely separated in their practices, they are deeply unified in principle.
A few of the more obvious characteristics include: A recognition that there
is much more to life than the material; a deep concern for the environment;
a commitment to equality and authenticity; a devotion to physiological
and spiritual development; and a recognition of relationship and
Wholeness to all life. These defining factors, and others, indicate that there
are millions more of us than we ordinarily recognize.

Perhaps it is time for those of us who know that the world is both spiritual and whole to admit we are bearers of light to a world that needs us
tremendously. Many of us have allowed each other and ourselves to carry
on in a deep sleep of conformity, materialism, and separation, and it is not
only suffocating our true essence, it is destroying the world at the same
time. There is a Native American saying that goes, "The one you have been
waiting for is you." Obviously, if you made it to the end of this chapter,
your spirit has led you to here and now. The question is: What's next?

Chapter Two

BEYOND POSITIVE THINKING: HOW IT ALL WORKS

Once upon a time, an ancient Indian king became obsessed with discovering the essence of Spirituality. "What is It? How can I find It? What should I do with It when I do find It?" Day after day, these questions bothered him. Intellectuals throughout his kingdom were offered a handsome reward to answer the king's questions. Many tried but none succeeded. At last, someone suggested the king consult a guru who lived just outside the borders of his kingdom.

"He is an old man and very wise," the king was told. "If anyone can answer your questions, he can."

The king went to the sage and posed the eternal questions. Without a word, the mystic went into his kitchen and brought out a grain of wheat.

"In this you will find the answer to your questions," the wise man said as he placed the grain of wheat on the king's outstretched palm.

Puzzled, but unwilling to admit his ignorance, the king clutched the grain of wheat and returned to his palace. He locked the precious grain in a tiny gold box and placed the box in his safe. Each morning upon waking, the king opened the box and examined the grain seeking an answer, but found nothing.

Weeks later, another guru passing through, stopped to meet the king who eagerly invited him to resolve his dilemma.

The king explained how he had asked the eternal questions but was given a grain of wheat. "I have been looking for an answer every morning but I find nothing."

"It is quite simple, your honor," said this new sage. "Just as this grain represents nourishment for the body, spirituality represents nourishment for the soul. If you keep this grain locked up in a gold box, it eventually perishes without providing nourishment or multiplying. However, if allowed to interact with the elements—light, water, air, soil—it will flourish and multiply, and soon you will have a whole field of wheat to nourish not only you, but many others. This is the meaning of practical spirituality. It must nourish your soul and the souls of others, and it must multiply by interacting with the elements."

WЬAT IS IT?

What happens after we wake up? Unfortunately, many of us act like the Indian king and attempt to put life's deepest questions and answers into a little box to study, observe, and control. I did something similar. After I woke up, I tried to learn everything I could about this new spirituality. As a good student, I signed up for every class, listened to many tapes, and read numerous books. Like the king, I wanted to believe that it was possible to know everything there was to know. Once I held the answers, then I would be in complete control and my life would be healthy, happy, prosperous, and nothing bad would ever happen. Right!

Now don't get me wrong, I learned and absorbed much in my studies and it was a good course of action. Every bit of it was a necessary part of my path. However, it is a mistake to believe that any of us can discover all the answers, especially in a short period. That is why we call It a Mystery.

What is "It" exactly? Some spiritual traditions claim that anything that can be named and described is not "It." However, while I acknowledge that I can never fully express the Unlimited Essence of the Universe, I still enjoy trying. It is superstition to believe that definitions could limit Spirit.

So keeping fully in mind that my portrayal of God defines me more than it defines the totality of God Itself, I believe that "It" is the manifest as well as the unmanifest aspect to all Life. If that sounds like everything, you're right. It is. It is everything we know and can even imagine, and It is more than that. It is everything invisible and what we conventionally think of as "spiritual," as well as everything material, and what we traditionally have called worldly. It is both what we think of as metaphysical, and what we may call profane. Everything. Todo. (That's Spanish for all!)

Okay, so if everything is It, what isn't It? Nothing! There is nothing that is not It. You could say that God is All There Is. Whoa! Wait a minute! Everything? That piece of trash laying in the gutter? The fly bouncing against the window trying to get outside? The World Trade Center, before and after? How can that be God? A better question is, if God is omnipotent, omniscient, and omnipresent, then how could any of it not be God?

If you take the time to study, you will discover that all of the world's religions have largely said the same thing. Unfortunately, when people get their opinions and judgments involved, we want to believe that God thinks the way we do, so we conceive of something besides God that creates and materializes Itself in ways we find undesirable. That is where evil comes from. There are certain expressions of God that are difficult to accept, so it is easier to come up with a different entity to blame, like the Devil, than to figure out how God could allow such a thing.

Maybe that is spiritual laziness. Or, maybe those explanations were useful for people and cultures that had not matured or were not capable of embracing the wholeness of God for whatever reason. Maybe someone wanted to control people, maybe not. For whatever reason, people throughout history have tried to put God in a tiny gold box and know all there was to know. They seem to prefer a tiny God in a little box that only did things that they could comprehend. That is certainly easier than embracing a God that is an unfolding, evolving Mystery.

But, if everything is God, what about those bad things? What about those things that happen in life that are clearly less than desirable? What about the thousands of innocent people who died in the World Trade Center? What about those 40,000 children worldwide who died today from malnutrition, and what about the horror of the Holocaust? Surely, God could not be a part of such tragedy?

It is difficult to imagine God being an element of all that when we think of God as merely a person. Yet, deny it as we might, that's what most of us do. We continue to think of God as one step above man. We limit the power and essence of the Universe to our human understanding. Thinking of God as a big giant or a Santa Claus, we put ourselves in the role of favored pets. It is easy and comforting to believe in that kind of God as long as we are the chosen ones in the family, and nothing bad happens.

I have a cocker spaniel and a cat. They definitely think of me as God, at least the dog does! I determine when and what they eat. If they are good, I tend to be loving and affectionate. If they do something to displease me, I scold them and withhold my affection. When there is tension in the house, they feel it. When there is joy and laughter, they feel that too. While they do have distinct personalities, their volition, or ability to affect their environment and life, is very limited and extremely dependent upon Thom and me.

People are not pets. We participate with life and thereby share in its creation. More than possessions of the Divine, or pawns of an absent parent, we are It. Remember, if it is all God, then how could we be anything less? If undesirable things happen on this planet, it is not because somebody or something is doing it to us, or even allowing it to happen. It is because we, collectively, are doing it to ourselves. God didn't destroy the World Trade Center, or let 40,000 children die of starvation today, or allow the Holocaust to exist. We did—and continue to do so. Humankind—sometimes individually and sometimes as a connected whole—created and so far continues to create the experiences we define as evil.

Does that mean that God is only a collection of humanity? Absolutely not. That too would be a limited definition. God is everything; hold that in your mind and mull on it. God is my dog and my cat (my cat knows this on a regular basis). God is also all the plants, all the animals, all the minerals, the water, in fact, the planet itself. However, God doesn't end there either. God is the Solar System, the Galaxy, the Universe, and everything beyond. A great metaphysical way to describe this is: God is both immanent (everything within me) and transcendent (everything outside and beyond me).

Consider that most everything I've just described is only the material aspect of God. Spirit includes everything invisible as well as everything in form. That means love, creativity, imagination, joy, and every other concept and attribute is It as well. My background in New Thought likes to explain this by saying that everything exists in the "mind" of God. Of course they aren't saying mind in the way we define brain, that would be a physical limitation. The Mind of God is a universal soup of possibility where everything invisible and visible exists, forever evolving. Another way of saying it is that God is a verb and not a noun.

Whew! And all you wanted was a simple definition of what It is! The problem with any simple definition is that people frequently forget that such descriptions are a short cut to the big picture. It is okay to define God in a simple way, but let's not make the mistake of believing that God is nothing more.

Also, keep in mind that although I use the word God liberally, that doesn't represent the God that you may have studied in your previously chosen religion. That's why you will find many in the New Thought and spiritual communities who just want to refer to God as "It" and stay completely away from the "G" word altogether. That's fine! It doesn't care. We can call It Harry, or Harriet, or Nothing at all. The only time we run into trouble is when we think that our way of describing It is the right and only way. If you haven't already noticed a few of my favorite words for It, is God, the Universe, Mind, Spirit, and anything else that I want to capitalize. Try it yourself.

δow δoes ɪτ woʀk?

Okay, so now we have a definition of It that includes everything. Then how does It work? A simple way to begin is to talk about my cousin Sammy.

As a kid, I avoided Sammy for two reasons: one, because he was a boy, and two, because he was always covered in dirt. There was a perpetual dark ring of grime around every fingernail, and frequently a faint line of dust encircling his mouth right where his lips met his face. Did he eat it too? Sammy scurried all over his parent's farm in scruffy overalls, and if he ever caught you in conversation, he'd ramble on about something he discovered in the garden that day. Only recently have I been able to look back and see him for the mystic that he was.

"You know what, Kathy?" he asked me one day when he caught me by surprise reading a book on the porch.

My look screamed, "Don't bother me!"

"No, you'll like this," Sammy said with a determined expression on his face. He sat down on the step nearest my patio chair and continued, "Did you know that if you plant a carrot, and take care of it, a carrot will grow."

"Oh, please," was my response. No wonder I avoided him.

"No, it's more than that," he continued undaunted. "If I plant beans, I get beans. If I plant corn, I don't get cucumbers, I get corn. Isn't that amazing?"

Now I was really fed up. It was one thing to humor the poor kid and another thing to listen to him make a fool of himself.

"What are you talking about Sammy?" I asked, not hiding my disgust. "Everyone knows that. Of course, we always get exactly what we plant. What's the big deal?"

"Oh," said Sammy as he slowly rose to his feet, his expression showing his doubt. "Silly me, I thought it was a miracle."

It is a miracle, Sammy. Yet, few of us remember how amazing the process actually is. What we plant, we reap. Whatever we plant—vegetables, ideas, concepts, fears, possibilities, whatever—that is what will grow in our garden. There is an undeniable factor to "It" that brings about the fruits of our thoughts. This is something we all know to the very core of our being, and yet on many occasions we act like I did with Sammy by saying, "What's the big deal?"

This isn't a new idea by any means. Over 2,600 years ago the Buddha said, "With our thoughts we make our world." Jesus said over 2,000 years ago, "It is done unto you as you believe." Ralph Waldo Emerson said, "We become what we think about all day long." Current spiritual teachers say it too. Deepak Chopra in his book, *The Seven Spiritual Laws of Success: A Practical Guide to the Fulfillment of Your Dreams* says, "Inherent in every intention and desire is the mechanics for its fulfillment." Author and speaker Wayne Dyer wrote a book entitled *You'll See It When You Believe It: The Way to Your Personal Transformation*. Of course, we know that what we plant, we grow, right?

Then why do we continue to expect different results? Huge numbers of us go through life planting things like doubt, worry, and fear and then wonder why we live lives of quiet desperation. We say we want to be happy, joyful, and fearless, yet we continue to focus our attention on the nightly news. If we recorded the words coming out of our mouths and the thoughts racing across our minds on any given day, we would see exactly the type of crop we plant on a regular basis. Want to know what you are planting? Then take a good hard look at your life.

So is that all God is? Is Spirit nothing more than a big clump of dirt? Again, it is good to remember that It can never be fully described. Defining God as a clump of dirt works as long as we realize that this aspect is only one of many attributes that we can utilize. Another way to think of It is as a cosmic soup of unlimited potential.

As a matter of fact, the science of quantum physics is proving on a regular basis that the material universe itself, at the subatomic level, responds to whoever is observing it, based upon the beliefs of the one who is doing the observing. Huh? What that means is that the world often responds to me according to what I believe is true. There it is again. If I go around believing that the world is a scary, unfriendly place, that is usually what I find. On the other hand, if I trust that people are intrinsically good and that good things happen to me all the time, I experience those good things on a regular basis.

Know anyone like that? I know a woman whom I'll call Dorothy who believes she lives in that kind of world. For her entire life, Dorothy dreamed of visiting the Dalai Lama. She saved for years and finally got the opportunity. Before leaving, she went to a new beautician to have her hair cut and styled for the trip. When she told Nancy, her new stylist, that she was going, Nancy asked, "You're going to India this time of year?" She then parted Dorothy's wet hair down the middle and pinned it up on the side before cutting. "Why would you ever want to go there? It's dirty, crowded, and the poverty is horrendous. Besides, the weather this time of year will be awful."

"Well, it's something I've always wanted to do," answered Dorothy. "Besides, a great part of the trip will be flying. I have reservations on India Air and I'll be flying in a 747. I've never flown in a jumbo jet and I can't wait."

"Oh no," said Nancy with a shake of her head, "I've heard India Air is a terrible airline. They have such old planes, it will be horribly cramped, and the flight takes hours. On top of that, I know of a woman who ate their food and got food poisoning. Be very careful what you eat! And where are you staying when you get there?"

"That's another great part of the trip!" said Dorothy with undeterred enthusiasm. "We'll be staying at a monastery near the Dalai Lama's residence. It's very well located and offers us a great vantage point for visiting all the temples and other sites."

"Oh dear," exclaimed Nancy as she snipped on Dorothy's hair. "I've heard about those monasteries. They are usually dirty with no running water. And the bugs! I've heard Buddhists never kill a bug, so the place is sure to be full of them."

"Well, the best part of the trip will be seeing the Dalai Lama," said Dorothy, ignoring the rebuff. "He is going to be present at a conference I'm attending." She watched Nancy in the mirror as she finished with the haircut and brought out the blow dryer.

"The Dalai Lama?" Nancy asked above the noise of the dryer. "It's practically impossible to understand him, let alone get anywhere close to him. Haven't you heard? You'll probably be stuck back in the corner somewhere." Nancy brushed out Dorothy's hair one last time and offered her a last piece of advice. "I suppose if you don't expect much, then you won't be disappointed."

A month later Dorothy passed Nancy on the street. They greeted one another and then Nancy asked, "So, how was your trip to India?"

"Actually," said Dorothy, "it was incredible. To begin with, the weather was wonderful. Each day the sun was shining and it was lovely and mild. All the locals were amazed at how perfect it was."

"What about your flight?" asked Nancy eagerly.

"Guess what?" Dorothy answered. "India Air purchased a new fleet of airplanes and we were the first to fly on that particular jumbo jet. It was such a popular flight that they sold out all the economy seats and we were miraculously upgraded to first class. The food and the service were awesome!"

"Okay, so what about that old monastery?"

"The monastery itself was simple but clean. In addition, the energy and feeling found there was the most peaceful and loving I've ever experienced. It rated about ten stars in my book, and…"

"What about the Dali Lama?" interrupted Nancy.

"Well," started Dorothy with hesitation. "We knew that it was going to be a bit crowded, so we decided to show up very early and take our chances. We got there several hours before the conference was scheduled to begin and found a place up near the front to sit. To our surprise, some monks came out and actually invited several of us in to meet with and talk to the Dalai Lama personally. Can you believe it?"

"You're kidding?" questioned Nancy. "You got to talk to the Dalai Lama in person?"

"Of course, we only got a few words. He's a very busy man you know."

"But what did he say," pressed Nancy.

"Well," answered Dorothy with hesitation. "He asked me where I got this terrible hair cut."

Okay, so maybe this story didn't happen exactly this way, but we've all known people like Dorothy who continue to expect good things, and they usually find them. We also have known people like Nancy who expect the worst, and things seem to go that way as well. The question is, which one are you?

In case you've noticed, Dorothy sounds a lot like Pollyanna. Unfortunately, most people only remember part of that tale. Many people like to say how unrealistic Pollyanna was and that couldn't happen in regular life. I say, go back and watch the movie again, and you will see that Pollyanna never denied that bad things happen. What she did do is refuse to focus on those negative things. She also didn't bury her head in the sand like an ostrich. Instead, she always looked for the good in every person and experience, and because she looked, she found it.

Still there is more to the process than that. It is one thing to say, "Just plant good things and good things happen." What occurs when you think you are planting good things and nothing seems to grow? What happens when something less desirable shows up?

First, check to make sure you are planting things properly. Remember, all plants need water and sunlight. Some even need a little fertilizer. If we don't provide our plants with the proper nourishment, they may take longer to grow and/or never reach maturity.

Planting things in Mind works very similarly. If you continue to hold an intention in your mind, staying clear and steadfast, there is a good possibility that idea will materialize in your life. Think about it. Most everything that now exists in the world first existed in someone's mind.

Say you want to buy a new home. First, you begin looking around and see what houses are available. You figure out how much of a home you believe you can afford. Some of this knowledge comes from support personnel like loan officers, and much of it comes from your own beliefs about yourself. Once you decide your price range, you begin to look at houses noticing things that you like and things you prefer to be different. Again, depending upon whether you believe you can afford and purchase the type of house you desire; you continue to search, continue to focus, until eventually a house of that description becomes available. You make an offer, you purchase the house, and eventually you move in.

Along the same lines, say you want a new job. First, you begin to imagine what type of job you would like to have. You begin to research the jobs available, discover what qualifications are necessary, begin to search the want ads, and eventually find a job similar to the one that you imagined.

Of course you can sabotage the process at any point. If you don't believe you deserve to buy a home, or can't afford it, nothing I tell you will convince you otherwise. If you think you are completely unqualified for the job of your dreams, you will never do what it takes to obtain it. If you think it is un-spiritual to have a nice home or work at a job you enjoy, then it is unlikely you will ever have those experiences. That's why I like to say, "you get to make it up."

In case you are wondering, prayer is an act of focused intention. While many who have been raised in a traditional religion may flinch at the word, the purpose behind it is similar. Prayer can help us to zero in on what is important to us, and then acknowledge the mysterious process in the Universe that brings it into being. I find it helpful to remember that when I pray it doesn't magically change things or people. What it does do is change me—my consciousness, and my beliefs. When those things change, circumstances outside of me change. If praying works for you, use it. If not, do it anyway, but call it something else.

Of course, the manifestation of our dreams isn't always easy, nor does it happen overnight. However, the process is reliable. When we plant the seeds of our beliefs with focus, intention, and continual energy, they eventually grow and thrive. Here are a few planting tips that can make the process go more smoothly.

• Remember everything has a season. If you plant carrots in the wintertime, you won't be growing carrots for some time to come. Winter is a time of rest and contemplation. It may be the time of year we just let things flow and see what shows up. While Spirit doesn't withhold from us, there is a season for everything. Getting in tune with nature and our place within it will affect our outcomes.

• Vegetables need water and sunlight, and our mental plants need nourishment too. The sorts of nourishment our spiritual plants need are focused attention and energy. It is one thing to set around daydreaming about the perfect job, and another thing to actively involve yourself in the process. There is an old saying that goes, "It works, if you work it." While we don't make a vegetable grow, our participation is essential.

• Depleted soil needs fertilizer (especially the natural kind). In the garden of Mind, the fertilizer we use has much to do with our environment and our consciousness. If you have a dream that you want to grow, you are highly advised to hang out with the type of people who will encourage you and support you. Then read stories and watch examples of others who have done what you are attempting to do to assure yourself that your dreams will come to fruition. Fertilizer is the passion and enthusiasm you feel for your dreams. If you animate your garden with that kind of emotional energy, it will be super charged with an extra boost.

• Protect your plant from predators. Just as there are insects and animals that will find your garden tasty, so too are there people who will nibble away at your dream until it loses life. While they may feel justified, we have a duty to our vision to protect it against invasion. Again, there are natural remedies. Simply refuse to discuss your dream around those who will not encourage or support you. Protect your plants, especially while they are young. As they mature, they will be able to withstand more obstacles, but never assume that they don't need your constant care.

• Keep weeds from overtaking your plant. Weeds are similar to predators but slightly different. They are the information that we will be tempted to read and then absorb that will discourage us or tell us why the experience of our dream is difficult or unlikely. If we want to start a business and yet watch the bad news on TV each night declaring the state of the economy, we are letting weeds grow in our garden. Turn it off! Refuse to read or expose yourself to negative information of any kind.

• Don't pull up the plant before its ready to harvest. It is tempting while your plant is young to pull it out to check on it. That's a big no-no. Don't judge the success of the plant by its size or by the rate of growth, and don't try to rush it. Planting is a mystical business and even though scientists can postulate and formulate many things, the mystery of what actually causes something to grow is beyond human understanding. Just know that what you plant in Universal Mind is growing and maturing in its own way. Trust it, feed it, take care of it, and chances are good that you will reap a bountiful crop.

• What if you discover you are growing something you don't really want? Great. If you realize that you don't like some of the experiences in your life, you can begin to change them. The benevolent aspect of the growth process says that if you change what you are planting, you can have a different result. While it might not be easy, or happen immediately, it will change. Remember, you get to make it up.

• What happens when it just won't grow? There are those in the New Thought community who refuse to even ask this question, believing that by asking we are planting the possibility of failure. I disagree. Sometimes what we want just doesn't happen. It may be that we don't get the house we thought we wanted, the loved one that we adored chooses another, or we get sick. Things happen. We may have set our intentions, followed all the suggestions, prayed our hearts out, and still things turn out differently.

In that instance, I believe that our Highest Self has a better idea in store for us. While most of the time you can plant a carrot, there will always be times when carrots just won't grow. It is beyond explanation. Sure, we can try to figure it out, and maybe an adjustment can be made here or there, but God remains a mystery that is always beyond our complete understanding. For that reason, sometimes it is best to wait and see what other good things Spirit has planned for us. Remember, any definition of God that lets you put It into a box and know everything about It by taking a workshop, is not omniscient, omnipotent, and omnipresent.

That reminds me of a man named Larry, who was relaxing in his home when it began to rain heavily. Nevertheless, Larry was without fear. All those spiritual classes he took and books he read told him that what he focused on was likely to occur. As the rains and the water rose, Larry continued to move higher and higher in his house until he found himself out on the roof. For blocks around, all he saw was water and other rooftops. Even still, Larry remained determined that a miracle would happen and he could stop the rain.

Then out beyond the steady pounding of the water Larry heard a motorboat approaching. Inside were two men who called out, "Come on mister, it's just getting worse. We can save you!" However, convinced that his solution was better, Larry stood, smiled, and waved them away. Shaking their heads, the rescuers motored off in search of other people to help.

Next, Larry heard a whirring noise and through the mist he saw a helicopter slowly making its way through the neighborhood. As it came closer, Larry saw a ladder flapping in the wind and he heard the pilot over a loud speaker, "Come on mister, this is your last chance." Once again, proud and determined, Larry sat down, shook his head, and waved the helicopter on its way.

The rain continued to fall; the water rose, and eventually washed Larry, his house, and his conviction away. Next, he found himself standing at the gates of heaven. He immediately began arguing with St. Peter. "I need to talk to God right now!" Larry exclaimed. "I set my intentions, I trusted that Spiritual Law would manifest, and now look what happened to me. What I want to know is: where was God in all this?"

St. Peter just shook his head sadly as he looked at the clipboard in his hand. "Larry, who do you think sent the boat and the helicopter?"

There is a power in the Universe that responds to our thoughts. We are not separate from it. While we don't make It happen or control It, we can, and do, co-create with It. Now that we have an idea of what It is and how It works, let's see how we can apply It in our everyday lives.

Chapter Three

MONDAY MORNING SPIRITUALITY: UNMASKING GOD AT WORK

It is one thing to say that God is everything, and we reap what we sow, and quite another to hear that alarm go off on Monday morning and drag ourselves up and out of bed for another day of work. Do we have to live in a monastery to be spiritual? Of course not! Is there a place for God on the job? Absolutely. The Spiritual is always present, although we habitually forget.

This doesn't just apply to those who go to a workplace either. I'm referring to any type of occupation. Be it a mother, homemaker, self-employed business owner, artist, writer, executive, professional, CEO—anything. Right there where you are, wherever and however you spend your primary time and energy each day, God is present and available. While we may think we are alone, separate, and struggling to survive, Spirit stands patiently within and beside allowing us the freedom to see if we like creating a life separate and alone with limited resources. If you're anything like me, eventually you discover that life is much easier as a partnership.

Now I'm not talking about any traditional type of God partnership, where you turn over everything to a big Cheese in the sky. I'm talking about a true co-creative relationship. As Miester Eckhart, the 17th Century mystic said, "God needs us as much as we need God." This means that the power and creative energy of the Universe sits, waits, and anticipates our conscious participation in all that is created. This is true especially at work.

Remember, the Spirit that I refer to is a process of Life, a fundamental essence of All That Is. This Life Force is a connecting glue that gives all our endeavors unlimited potentiality. While we may achieve a great deal of success on our own, it is only after we choose to consciously align with the unlimited nature of Possibility that we achieve our highest potential.

My own path to reaching this understanding took time. When Thom and I first set foot on the metaphysical path, we were drawn to the idea of the Universe helping us to succeed. You may recall that back in the 80's we, and everyone we knew, were obsessed with getting rich. We had achieved only fleeting success by the time we reached our mid-thirties, and when we heard of the uplifting message to be found in an unlimited idea of God, our minds hooked into it in a convenient way.

Guess what? It made a difference. Not in any major or dramatic way, but in small and subtle avenues. We began making decisions that were more congruent with our personalities and our life purposes. We stopped obsessing over the quick fix and began to search for lifetime solutions to our well being. We let go of our previous attempts to find short cuts to happiness and wealth, and gradually learned to focus our attention on making conscious choices that would lead to a future of satisfaction and happiness.

For example, in the late 1980's, we moved to the Palm Springs area of Southern California. At the time, we had a small savings in the bank and no jobs. Our background was real estate sales, so it was easy for Thom to find a job with a commercial real estate company and begin working. However, keep in mind that real estate pays by commission only, so there was no immediate salary or income in sight. Commercial real estate is more specialized than residential, so income tends to be even more unpredictable.

Although Thom and I had both attended metaphysical classes through Religious Science for several years by that time, our lack of income frightened me. However, Thom held fast and refused to go out and get another kind of job just to bring in money. Even though part of me agreed with him, especially on spiritual principle, I still couldn't shake my fear.

As a solution, I applied to work at a temporary employment agency. With a varied employment background I rated $10 an hour. I was immediately assigned a position as an administrative assistant in a hotel in their food service department. While the work was somewhat interesting, and certainly not drudgery, it was obvious that the only reason I was there was because I thought I needed the income.

After two weeks I knew I had to quit. I was deeply unhappy and becoming increasingly resentful of my husband. After all, what gave him the right to do what he wanted and not go out and make money like me? If I had to sell my soul, shouldn't he? We sat down and had a long heart-to-heart talk.

"Kathy," he said, "I love you and I care about our future. But there is no way I am going to go out and work at a job I hate just to make money. I like commercial real estate, I think I'm pretty good at it, and I'm going to stick it out."

"But what about our bills?" I asked, not liking the whine I heard in my own voice.

"We'll figure something out," he answered. Then he took my hand and looked into my eyes, "The real question is, why do you think you have to work at a job you hate to make money? Haven't we learned that we get to make it up?"

I could feel a shift inside me. Here he was courageously doing what he wanted to do, and operating from the belief that we deserve to be able to work at a job that we love. Why was I not doing the same? Fear, it was plain and simple fear. I carried around a belief that people have to do things they dislike in this world. That old conviction, grounded in fear and transgression, said that it didn't matter what would make my heart sing. Survival demanded I do whatever necessary to get by. A new belief, fragile but growing, said different. If the Universe really responds to us according to our beliefs, then I could choose to have a job I loved, and make good money doing it.

Once I was able to see and think about work in a new way, I asked for

Thom's help in creating something new. Together we sat at the kitchen table and began a list. What was it that I had a natural ability to do?

• I was good on the computer. I learned through other business work about layout, design, mailing lists, and advertising.

• I was great at organizing things. I can multi-task with the best of them.

• I had a real estate broker's license, and although I abhorred selling, I did enjoy the knowledge and information gathering aspect of it.

Then Thom asked me straight out, "What is it that you love to do?"

My answer was simple enough, "I like to write, I like to create, and I like sharing ideas. I also enjoy the freedom of making it up my own way."

After that, we made an inventory of the things that we owned that I could use if I were to create a new business. We had a computer, a fax machine, and a telephone.

It was that unpretentious. Once we had this information down on a piece of paper we asked ourselves: what can I do with this collection of talents, desires, and hardware that will allow me to create? What parts of my past can I use to develop something I love? What could I do that didn't need a lot of capital to start, other than what we already had? What service could I provide to others, that no one else was providing? Within one or two hours, we had developed a business in which I would write and publish a monthly newsletter as an advertising piece for escrow, mortgage, and title insurance companies within California.

Within a year, I supplied over ten companies with monthly newsletters and my business began supporting our family financially. While it didn't happen immediately, it flowed in an amazingly synchronistic way. Of course there were several bumps along the path, too. One was in the area of pricing. With no idea how to price my product, I researched what professional writers charged for something similar. Although it seemed high, I became determined to prove the principle that the Universe responds to our beliefs and gives us what we think we deserve. I asked for the going rate for writers, and never once have I been questioned about my rates.

Another hurdle was our willingness to trust the process and finance ourselves as the business grew. Our income was very low for the first six months to a year, and many of our bills were paid on credit. Although it was necessary for us to be conservative in our expenses, and it took time, we eventually paid off the debt and began to operate in the black. I am proud to say that after twelve years I am still the writer and publisher of that newsletter business. Not only has it supported my family very well, but it also paid me to learn how to be a much better writer, and gave me the freedom and ability to create in numerous ways.

There is absolutely no doubt in my mind that you, and everyone else, could do exactly the same thing. Obviously your talents and experience offer you a different and unique recipe, but there is something out there for you as well. The truth is, each of us receives what we believe we deserve. No more and no less. Spirit will mirror back to you whatever you believe regarding your work. Think you have to work at a job you hate? Guess what? You're absolutely right! The Universe says, "Yes!" Think you get to work at a job you love and make good money doing it? Guess what? You're right too! The Universe says yes to you too!

I have friends who say, "But you don't know my profession." The best answer for them is an old metaphysical saying that goes, "Argue for your limitations and they're yours." In other words, if you believe your skills or profession are so unique that you can't make it up your way, then you are absolutely right! Remember, the Universe just says, "Yes!"

I have other friends that say, "But I don't have any talents." I disagree. While you may not be aware of your talents, you do have them. Every single person on this planet has been given a unique and special collection of tendencies that are either developed or undeveloped. What made me think of newsletters? Actually, I had written newsletters for the real estate convention I previously worked for, and I had volunteered at the church we attended by writing their monthly newsletter for over a year. It was something I had already been willing and able to do; I just took it a step further.

If you go back and look into your past, you'll see little seeds of possibilities that repeatedly popped up in your life.

Of course, you can't go from zero to sixty overnight. While I held the dream of writing books for almost twenty years, and achieved minor successes along the way, this is my first published book. The published articles, the newsletters, and the other manuscripts I wrote were necessary education to this point. Remember, before you graduate, you have to attend elementary school. A person doesn't play Carnegie Hall without many years of practice.

Then I have other friends who say, "But I can't leave my job because I make way more money doing this than living my dream." That is a common excuse for many in my generation. Some of us have been on the corporate ladder climb for years and although we are bored and unhappy with what we do, we get satisfaction from the amount of money we make. Because of that income, we have high expenses, and have grown comfortable with a lifestyle we aren't sure we want to give up.

A friend named Rachel was caught in this particular dilemma a few years ago. Rachel lived on the east coast and worked in downtown Manhattan. Although proud of her income, proficiency, and position at a large pension fund company, the personal cost to her and her family was high. Long work hours, stress, and a three to four hour commute from her home in Princeton, New Jersey, each and every day, carried a toll.

Thom met Rachel while working on a transaction concerning a large commercial real estate property owned by her company. After several interactions, they became friends, and when Thom and I traveled to New York City, we visited Rachel and her husband Rob, and got to know them even better. Rob worked at home on his own Internet company. They owned a great house in Princeton in an excellent neighborhood and drove a new Volvo. By all appearances, they were a successful, upwardly mobile couple.

While obviously proud of their achievements, we heard a longing in their voice for something different. Our conversations touched on many things, including metaphysics, and before long we were sharing some of the stories of life as we now saw it. We talked about the freedom and joy to be found in living where we loved to live and working at things we loved doing. They admitted, they too, wanted to move to California, and agreed it would be awesome to work at something that incited their passions. However, they had a long list of excuses of why that wasn't possible.

Even after we returned home, the conversation continued. Whenever Thom made a business call to Rachel, she would consistently refer to her dreams for a new business and a move to California. Thom sent her a book about the integration of spirit and business, and Rachel told him that she read it often as she traveled back and forth on the train to work. Daily the commute seemed longer, the job more stressful, and her time away from her husband more painful.

During one phone conversation, Rachel admitted she was very close to quitting her job. Each day it became more of a reality as she and Rob talked. Then one morning Thom got an email from Rachel. It said, "THE BASTARDS GAVE ME A RAISE."

Sure enough, sensing her growing dissatisfaction, her superiors had increased her salary with the hopes that it would lure her back into trading her life for more money. It worked—for a while. It took almost another year before she and Rob made the break. They are now living in Southern California, but it wasn't easy. It seems that the more you think you have to lose, the less you may be willing to give it up. Their desire for comfort and money was very strong, almost strong enough to make them think it was worth sacrificing their souls.

So did they lose much by making the change? It depends upon what you think is valuable. While they still live very comfortably, there were adjustments. If you base the merit solely on what they own and how much money they have in the bank, then yes, they have had to conserve. But, if you value things like living in a place and a location you like, spending many more hours with the ones you love, having the freedom to do things your own way and in your own time, finding something you love doing to contribute to the world, then they are now far ahead of the game. On top of that, they are certainly living closer to their life's purpose.

There is another aspect of spirituality at work to address. Even if you can accept that you deserve to have a job that excites you and brings you a sufficient income, there are those that say it is impractical to mix business with spirit. In this area, Thom remains one of my greatest examples. In the highly competitive area of commercial real estate sales, he repeatedly challenges himself with the idea that he "gets to make it up." To the best of his ability, he refuses to be drawn into aggressive power struggles, competition, or the continual temptation to act unethically. With high standards for his own self-expression, his income and reputation for quality grows each year.

Thom says that his trust and peace increases to the extent that he lets go of fear. Fear, of course, is not that someone or something will harm him, but rather the more insidious kind that says someone or something is out to take away his good. Fear says if he doesn't close this deal, or if he loses that client, then he will suffer great loss. Yet, as long as he remembers that his belief largely affects the outcome, and that no one is the enemy, the fear melts away and he is able to act from his Spirit. This is a daily challenge that every one of us face (Thom and I included!) as we go through life. Work, or our creative expression, is one of the primary areas in which this principle is tested.

Keep in mind that doing something you love doesn't mean that you just kick back and do nothing. Life is seldom a free ride. The choice isn't whether we participate, only how. When we freely offer our gifts, passions, and dreams, the Universe co-conspires with us in their achievement. If we just sit on our butts, all we get is a bigger one. Remember, in work and just about everything else that we do, we usually get what we give.

I won't pretend that it is always easy for either Thom or me. Some days we do better than others. I am also very aware that certain people have more to overcome. It may even appear to you in terms of environment, education, childhood, physical limitations, and self-esteem that you have been unfairly challenged and have too much to rise above. However, my observation is that a large number of those who started out above me, and have climbed high, frequently find that their ladder is leaning against the wrong wall. Just because someone has more toys than you, a more prestigious job, lots of initials behind their name, or more money in the bank, doesn't mean that they are anywhere nearer to finding true peace and happiness. The problem is that most of us have been playing a game by someone else's rules. It is time to change the game as well as the rules.

Whether you agree with me, or not, about if you can work at a job you love while making good money, is up to you. Either way, you get to make it up. Remember, if you argue for your excuses, they are yours. My story shows how this works when you are at the end of your rope and just struggling to survive. Rachel's example shows what happens when you think you have a lot to lose. Thom's experience demonstrates it can be achieved, even in a highly competitive environment. When all is said and done, we are here to express and co-create with a Universe that just says, "Yes!"

Here is another way of looking at it:

An American investment banker wandered out on the pier of a small coastal Mexican village when a little boat with just one fisherman came into the dock. Inside the unimpressive boat lay several large yellow fin tuna.

"Wow, those look great," commented the American. "How long did it take to catch them?"

The dark-skinned man replied, "Only a little while."

"But it's early. Why didn't you stay out longer and catch a lot more fish?" asked the American with a mind clearly working overtime.

The Mexican man explained he had enough to support his family's immediate needs.

The American then asked, "But what do you do with the rest of your time?"

The fisherman replied, "I sleep late, fish a little, play with my children, take siesta with my wife Maria, and stroll into the village each evening where I sip wine and play guitar with my amigos. I have a full and busy life."

The American scoffed. "I am a Harvard MBA and can help you. I recommend you spend the entire day fishing and with the proceeds buy yourself a bigger boat. With that income, you could buy several bigger boats, so that eventually you could have a fleet of fishing boats. In addition, instead of selling your catch to an intermediary, you should sell directly to the processor and could eventually open your own cannery. Then you would control the product, processing, and distribution. With that in place you would need to leave this small village and move to Mexico City, then LA, and eventually NYC where you will run your expanding enterprise."

"The Mexican man asked, "But, how long would that take?"

To which the American answered, "Oh, 15 or 20 years."

"Then what?" asked the fisherman.

The American laughed and said. "That's the best part. When the time is right you would announce an IPO and sell your company stock to the public and become a very, very rich man. You'd make millions."

"Millions?" asked the fisherman. "Then what?"

"Then what?" returned the American. "Then you could retire. You'd move to a small coastal fishing village where you would sleep late, fish a little, play with your kids, take siesta with your wife, and stroll into the village in the evenings where you could sip wine and play your guitar with your amigos."

Chapter Four

MONEY: TRUE ABUNDANCE MEANS MORE THAN DRIVING A MERCEDES

I once heard a story about a God and a Goddess like the ones in the old Sinbad movies that wore exotic Arabian outfits and sat on clouds gazing down on the doings of humans. One day this Godly couple watched a beggar as he wandered down a road far below them. His clothes were tattered and torn, his beard was ragged, and his bare feet bloody.

With compassion, the Goddess frowned in sympathy at the sight of this destitute man, and shook her head at his plight. "Oh darling," she sighed, and said to her beloved sitting next to her, "Look at that poor human. Can't we do something?"

"Now my dear," the God answered with affection, "you know we aren't allowed to play favorites. The man must make his own destiny."

"But darling," the Goddess insisted, "he's calling out our name in prayer. He's asking for a share of our abundance. How can we deny him?" She flitted out her jewel covered hand and swept through the air emphasizing the extent of their kingdom.

"Honey, I know you are sympathetic, it is part of your power. Still, it wouldn't do him any good; it's against spiritual law. You can't give someone something they are not ready to receive."

Not content with his answer, the Goddess continued to press her partner for a solution to the beggar's poverty, as she watched from the clouds above. Finally, out of his love for his wife, the God agreed. With a wave of her hand, a large bag of gold materialized out of thin air. With another flutter, the bag of gold dropped out of the heavens and landed several yards in front of the beggar on the dirt road.

The beggar had been walking down this particular road all day. His stomach growled with hunger, his eyes were crusty with dirt from the road, and his throat was parched from whispering prayers to the Gods all day long, "Please dear God, shower me with your abundance. All I ask is that you give me the money to take me out of my poverty. Then I'll be happy. Have mercy on me, please dear God." On and on, his prayer rolled off his dusty lips. With eyes closed, he walked on.

So involved was he with his prayer that he nearly tripped when he stubbed his toe on a large rock laying right in the middle of the road. It briefly broke his concentration, so much so, that his prayer changed its tune. "Ouch! Damn it! You'd think with all the traffic on this road there wouldn't have to be rocks at all!" With a sigh, he closed his eyes and returned to his prayers.

Overhead the Goddess watched as the beggar stumbled over her bag of gold and walked on. She looked over at the God beside her, who only nodded his understanding at the silliness of humans.

No one can give us anything we don't believe we deserve. In fact, no one can give us anything that isn't ours by right of consciousness. Our finances frequently make this very obvious. Remember, the Universe always agrees with our conscious and unconscious thoughts and beliefs. Whatever you think about money, God just says, "Yes!"

An entire chapter about money in a book about spirituality may seem odd, but those who live in the real world know it is an issue many address every day. After all, just try acting spiritual when you are struggling to pay your rent, or if your credit card bills are way past due, or if your child is very sick and you have no insurance. Practical spirituality says there is something you can do about your finances. Things can change. As a co-creative partner with the unlimited potential of the Universe, it is possible to live in financial harmony on the inside, as well as the outside. You might not ever become rich, but you can feel abundant. Isn't it the feeling we're after anyway?

Have you ever heard that water rises to its own level? That is a very basic way of saying that if you have so much water, it will always return to that level regardless of the amount of times you displace it. The same is true of money. Money always rises and falls to the level of our consciousness, or our deeply held convictions. What that means is that even if you win the lottery, even if old Aunt Gertrude leaves you a fortune, you will eventually return to having about the same amount of money as you had before. On the other hand, if you lose a significant amount of money, or have to pay off a large debt, your finances will eventually find their way back to your level of money consciousness. The only way things change, money included, is if something inside us changes.

A great example of this occurred in my own life. Many years ago, Thom became indirectly involved in a real estate lawsuit that was, in our opinion, completely without merit. It was a shotgun lawsuit where everyone involved was named for huge sums of money. This lawsuit hung over our heads for nearly seven years. It eventually went to a trial that lasted three months, and then after a mistrial was declared, another couple of years passed. The experience contained many lessons for our family, including the intimidating possibility of a judgment of over $1 million. Finally, the opportunity came to settle the entire ordeal for $20,000. While remaining certain of Thom's innocence, the opportunity to end the experience was a choice we both agreed to take. We borrowed the money, and paid the $20,000 with a sense of overwhelming relief that the anxiety was over.

Interestingly enough, the money we borrowed was never a burden. By surrendering to the lesson of the experience, by trusting that "all would be well" without fight or resentment, the incident seemed to disappear.

Almost overnight, unexpected business transactions arrived out of nowhere allowing us to repay the debt within a few months. Not only were we mentally free, our consciousness was set at a certain level, and the payment on the lawsuit was little more than a momentary displacement of that level. Our lifestyle never changed a bit. The metaphysical principle behind this lesson was, "No one can take anything from you that is yours by right of consciousness."

Can a person really live this way? Can a person live in the "real world" knowing that your consciousness determines your income? Yes. Your job, the economy, your education, and your environment, are simply the avenues your consciousness uses to direct income to you. Where does money come from? Wherever it is now. Remember, if everything is God, then money is God too. It shifts, rearranges, and manifests itself, much like energy, according to belief. What you believe about money reflects itself in the state of your consciousness. Want more money? Then work primarily on your consciousness.

I'm just like most of you. I was raised to believe that by getting the right education, networking, following the right career path, associating with the right people, and with a lot of hard work and luck, I'd make lots of money.

I now know there is another way. By spending half the time building and developing a consciousness of abundance, instead of spending all the time that we do following the traditional path to getting rich, we would all be further ahead, and happier.

Why do I believe that? Mainly because my life has been such an example. I have already confessed that Thom and I spent much of the first ten years of our marriage running after success. It seemed the more we ran, the faster it ran, and was always just out of reach. Once we got involved in metaphysics, we began to understand many of the reasons why wealth continued to elude us.

Both Thom and I were raised in working class families. We were both taught to work hard and not expect too much. Thom, particularly, grew up in a very traditional Christian fundamentalist household where he learned that you were actually closer to God when you didn't have much money. We were both programmed with the idea that money couldn't make you happy, and often would do exactly the opposite.

At the same time, our society teaches us early on that the American Dream is more than just owning our own home; it is getting rich and buying everything we want. For many years Thom and I heard voices within us telling us that money wasn't good and the root of all evil, while advertisements everywhere continued to sell us on the fact that money was the answer to everything. You can imagine the confusion!

Thinking we could drown out the voices inside, we plunged into the world of getting rich quick. In the early 1980's we began to buy and sell homes and rental properties in Colorado Springs, Colorado. As real estate brokers, we got by fairly well, but any real wealth seemed just out of reach. In 1985, we assembled an elaborate real estate transaction that appeared to be the answer to everything. Unable to finance it on our own, we brought on partners to secure the deal. After only a few short months, following the betrayal and embezzlement of one of our partners, the entire dream collapsed.

This apparent failure inspired a move back to Southern California. However, instead of moving to the desert where our hearts wanted us to be, we moved to the greater Los Angeles area in pursuit of (you guessed it) money. Money continued to elude us until we began to study spirituality. Gradually we learned that instead of listening to what the world and others told us we needed, we should instead look and listen within. Then we really began to uncover the baggage we had about money.

One by one, we unearthed our fears and limitations regarding money. Slowly, and I do mean slowly, we changed those underlying core beliefs. Let me be very blunt when I say that it takes time to change your deeply held convictions. A one-weekend workshop won't do it, much as we tried to make it happen ourselves! Depending upon your level of financial awareness to begin with, you first have to work to root out what you presently believe, and then transform those ideas with a knowingness about money that serves you. Consciousness is more than just saying you agree with something, or that you even believe something. Consciousness is a conviction about something held deeply within; it is a "becoming" something.

On the other hand, even if you rev up your money awareness, that does not necessarily mean you are more spiritual. Evidence is everywhere that having money, and/or having the consciousness of money, does not prove you have a consciousness of love, compassion, or wholeness. In the end, what we do with our money, what we think about money, and whether we own it, or it owns us, tells us what we believe about the world and ourselves.

In other words, money and the other effects in our lives are just by-products of who we think we are and why we are here. In the big picture of life, each of us is a magnificent, unlimited, and eternal expression of the God Force. Because this Force always responds to us according to what we believe, money and other effects show up as a natural reflection of a creative and giving nature. Again, we always get what we give.

A perfect example of that is how Thom's and my money consciousness actually matured and blossomed when we surrendered our old focus for something completely new. Eight years ago, when we began devoting a significant portion of our time, energy, and money to co-creating a spiritual community, something seemed to shift within us. By switching the dedication of our life from getting things and having things, to being of service to others and the world, money seemed to take care of itself. It wasn't like we planned it by saying something like, "Oh, if we do this, the Universe will reward us." It was simply a change of priorities. Once we changed, the Universe seemed to acknowledge our new consciousness by saying, "You're right, money is not something you need to worry or fuss about anymore. You just do what you came here to do, and leave the rest to me." Since that time, we have lived an increasingly affluent and fulfilling life.

So how does one go about creating a consciousness of money that exists congruently with a spiritual life? Here are a few ideas.

• Remember: It is done unto you, as you believe. What you think about money, what you believe about money, that pattern will be reflected in your life. When you accept that awareness, then most of the other steps will be easier.

• Have patience. Remember it took a long time for you to believe what you presently believe about money, so, it will take time for your money ideas to change.

• Be inner-directed, not outer-directed. Part of the confusion about money happens because we listen to what the world says about money and ignore the beliefs we hold inside. Pay no attention to what other people, the TV, your parents, and society says about money. Become brutally honest with what you believe about money and then bravely hold those beliefs up to the light of Spirit.

• Keep studying. Take classes and workshops. Sure you can focus on ideas of abundance and money, but don't stop there. As your view of life and the beliefs you hold become clearer, you will be changing many things. Money is only one of them. As you develop into a more wholistic, compassionate, loving, and interconnected being, your money issues will automatically be adjusted.

• Think of money as another form of energy. Your new consciousness will constantly remind you that wherever you put your energy, that thing or experience grows. So when you put your money out, realize you are "voting with your dollars." If you hoard your money, or are stingy, you tell the Universe that there is not enough to go around. The Universe says, "Yes!" If you spend your money wisely, supporting people, organizations, and businesses that support you and the world, then you are freely sharing an unlimited Source that will continue to flow back to you.

• Your past does not determine your future. This idea extends to all areas of your life. Today is a new day and anything that has not worked for you in the past can change from this time forward.

• Give yourself away. I've learned that the only time I don't think I have enough, is when I feel I'm not enough. If you become the person that you are meant to be, and if you dedicate yourself to giving yourself to others and all Life, you will probably discover, as I did, that you can't out-give God.

You may be saying to yourself, "Well sure, these ideas sound pretty good, but does it really work?" Take my word for it, it might not always be easy, but it is possible. Both Thom and I are self-employed professionals where each month we must rely on the Universe for income. We can either choose to believe that we've just been lucky, or alternatively, that the Universe is our Source. We can believe that one client or another can make or break us, or we can choose to believe that we have an infinite supply of abundance available to us at all times. We decide. What we put our attention on grows.

Unfortunately, many people believe that their particular job holds the purse strings to their finances. Then if their employer decides to fire them or penalize them, they feel completely helpless and victimized. Some believe their good fortune depends upon the economy, and then if it takes a downturn, they once again feel out of control and powerless. As long as you tie your income to something outside yourself, be it a job, your boss, the economy, or Aunt Gertrude, then you will constantly feel like a puppet with someone else pulling the strings. Your finances are always up to you.

When your good lies solely within your consciousness and its relationship with the Universe, then even if you experience a setback in your finances, you will see it in an optimistic light. When you believe God works for you and with you, then every money experience, up or down, can teach you something amazing and wonderful about yourself, and it can lead to even greater understanding in the future. When money becomes an inside-out job, then you'll never feel like a victim again.

While it remains a challenge to not become attached to any one person, company, or channel of income, it can be done. The most important thing you can do is to surround yourself with people who believe the same way you do, who live that way themselves, and who will help remind you of your true Source. Once you can make the shift in your consciousness to knowing this as true, you will achieve a degree of peace regarding your finances that you could never have imagined.

People also appear to have a lot of judgment about the flow of money. What I mean is that some people seem to believe that if they have one type of occupation that brings in money, versus another, then somehow that income is more spiritual. Remember, money is nothing more than an energy and a reflection of your beliefs. To judge that some money is good and other money is less than good, gives it an innate power that it does not have. Remember, if you get to make it up, your profession is as holy as you are. Any income you obtain from your work is as spiritual as the energy and consciousness you hold.

To live in the real world and hold down any kind of occupation where you do it with mindful awareness, a sense of connection to the Universe, and a giving attitude of service, is about as spiritual as it gets. It doesn't matter if you are a waiter, a minister, a mom, a gardener, or a doctor. Perhaps if we all worked towards that kind of relationship in whatever we did, then money would take care of itself and our jobs would be a source of inspiration, nourishment, and healing. And money? Money would rightfully return to being merely a byproduct of the good we do in the world.

Another thing I've noticed about money is that it brings up competition in many people. Besides judging whether we think our obtaining it is spiritual or not, we also tend to judge the quantity or productivity of it in a very unspiritual way. I think our culture indoctrinates us with this idea. We like to believe, and tell each other, that things that cost a great deal must be more valuable. Hence, we also believe that if you make more than me, then you must have more worth than me.

While this is usually an unconscious belief, ask any artist if they feel their art has value. Most of them will say, "Only if I can sell it, and then only as much as I can get." Ask any mother or homemaker how much they are worth and most of the time they will say, "Not much by the hour." Yet, few question when the CEO of a large corporation demands millions of dollars as his compensation. We value business in this culture much more than we value domestic or creative endeavors. We perpetuate that belief in each other, and believe it for ourselves. Unfortunately, we then have to live with that kind of limiting conviction. When we begin to reinforce in each other that any labor performed with love, service, and creativity is the most valuable that we can do, the world will be transformed.

Finally, one thing I did learn from my family about money is true. Money does not buy happiness. While it is difficult to find any true peace or satisfaction if you are hungry and if you have no place to sleep at night, once the basics are covered, the rest of our happiness is up to us.

I recently heard a story of a man who worked as a rug weaver. This simple man passionately enjoyed weaving rugs, and each day he sang, whistled, and passed the hours happily as he worked. Then at night, he walked to his little shack to sleep soundly. One day a rich man happened by and saw this impoverished weaver. Filled with compassion, the rich man gave him a hundred dollars. "Take this," he said, "and go enjoy yourself."

The basket weaver took the money with much awe. A hundred dollars was more money than he had ever seen in his whole life. He left work and went home to his dilapidated hut wondering where to keep it. Unfortunately, his shack was not secure. Worrying about thieves, or even rats nibbling at his cash, he didn't sleep at all that night.

The next day he carried his hundred dollars to work but he did not sing or whistle because he was still worried about securing the money. Once more that night he did not sleep. Finally, the next morning, he returned the hundred dollars to the wealthy man, saying, "Keep this, and give me back my happiness."

Chapter Five

RELATIONSHIPS:
OUR SPIRITUAL TEACHERS
WEAR MANY DISGUISES

Mark works in downtown Palm Springs, California. Because it is a resort community, displays awesome weather and is incredibly beautiful, new people move there continuously. Recently Mark met one of these new transplants as he sat eating his lunch at one of the many sidewalk cafes.

After introductions, the man sat down in a chair across the table. "Would you mind telling me a little about your town?" he asked.

"What would you like to know?" Mark asked between bites of his sandwich.

"Well, mainly I'd like to know what kind of people live here?"

"Sure," Mark answered. "First, can I ask what kind of people live in the town where you're from?"

"Actually, that's the main reason I moved. The people there were terrible. Not only were they rude and inconsiderate, but crime was awful. Both my car and my home were broken into on several occasions. Jobs were hard to find, and they paid practically nothing. I couldn't wait to get out of there. People told me this place had a lot going for it, so I thought I'd give it a try."

"Unfortunately, I have some bad news," said Mark sympathetically. "You're going to find exactly the same thing in this town."

The man nodded sadly as though he wasn't surprised Before long he headed off down the street and Mark never saw him again.

That very same day, Mark stopped in Starbucks for a cup of coffee. When he couldn't find a free table outside, he asked a young woman sitting alone if he could join her.

Before long, just as the man had done earlier that day, the young woman asked. "Maybe you could tell me a little bit about this town, Mark. I'm new and I'd really like to know what kind of people live here."

"First, tell me what type of people lived in the town where you're from," Mark asked as he sipped his cafe mocha.

"Actually, it was very difficult to leave. The people there were absolutely wonderful. If you needed anything there were always dozens of people to call. Everyone was warm and generous. I had a super job and lots of friends. The only reason I moved is because of a set of very synchronistic events. What I see here so far, I like."

"Funny thing," Mark answered with a smile, "you'll find that this town and its people are pretty much the same."

There it is again. What you think about, you bring about. No matter where you live, work, or go, you will find the same type of experiences and people that you find where you are. This fundamental principle is obvious, sometimes painfully so, in the area of our relationships. The only way things change is if we change.

Every relationship you have is a living, breathing, walking, feedback mechanism that offers you tremendous opportunities to get to know yourself and grow. Relationships offer one of the most down-to-earth avenues to practice your spirituality to greater and greater depths.

Amazingly, the old religious pattern was to avoid relationships. Many in the leadership roles were denied marriage, family, and little real world companionship. Monasteries and nunneries were set up to separate the religious from the everyday experiences most of the public knew. While that path may have proved beneficial for some, I think the state of the world today is an example of how most people need, and are seeking, something different. It is time to put the spiritual life into everyday living, and that means to embrace relationships as a direct path to the Divine.

FAMILY RELATIONSHIPS

The first relationships to address are those within our primary family. Mothers, fathers, siblings, and other assorted family members are all fodder for our personal and spiritual growth. Chances are if you are reading this book, you are an adult, so you no longer need your parents for survival. With that in mind, your familial relationships are now a matter of choice. "Choice?" you ask. "How can that be?" While you will always be the daughter or son or sibling to your birth family, regardless of your age, you are now an adult and your relationship with that family is a matter of your making. You get to make it up.

Of course, we often forget and frequently don't act that way. However, once we become adults and thereby self-sufficient, the way we interact with anyone in our family of origin is always our decision. Although I wasn't raised this way, from a larger perspective we are actually connected to every single person on this planet. Our genes are so much alike that there is only .1% difference between my genes and those of the 6.5 billion other people on this planet. That .1% is extremely small. What I do share with my family of origin is history. To the degree that I am tied to that history or that past, I am tied to my family. That tie remains a choice.

Now that we consciously know we have a choice about our family, is there any other reason to hang around those people for the rest of our lives? That answer is up to us. One answer may come from the question posed by Mark to the newcomers. "What were the people like in the family you come from?" I have noticed that the way we refer to our families, regardless of whether they were wonderful, or completely dysfunctional, usually tells us more about ourselves than the family we think we are describing.

For example, Thom's mother was an extremely religious woman and her very narrow interpretation of God had enormous effects on his young life. They attended church for many hours each week and things like movies, cards, and dancing were considered evil. After all our years of marriage, I have heard many stories of his early life and some bordered on abuse. If Thom wanted to trot out the dysfunction of his family as an excuse for some of his failings, most people would nod in sympathy.

However, I have heard just as many stories from Thom about other experiences in his life. While Thom and his mother had an on-going battle of wills throughout his childhood, he remembers one thing she told him very clearly. She said, "You can do anything you set your mind to." He has recalled that message many times in his life when he needed motivation, and in spite of his extreme religious training, the seeds of a very deep spiritual life were planted. He has never doubted the existence of God, only the packaging. Faced with a choice, Thom chooses to selectively remember the good things about his mother and his family.

As another example, I have three sisters and I think I can safely say each of us interprets our childhood and our parents in very different ways. What that indicates to me is that each of us sees our past and our family based upon our own personality, our beliefs, and our soul identity. Whatever story we individually tell about our family is our biography, not necessarily the others.

Once you are willing to start seeing your family as a story you are continually recreating, you can release them from your expectations. An ongoing problem with any family happens because we expect them to be, or do, something that they either can't or won't. While it has taken me many years, I've discovered that parents do not behave the way I think they should, and sisters do exactly what they want. The big question is: Do I let them, or do I fight to change them and thereby make me, and them, unhappy? Again, it is my choice.

The most practical and spiritual thing we can do with our family of origin is to love them and accept them for who they are. Who are they? Why, our teachers and guides! Our family either teaches us a great way to be, or they demonstrate a great way not to be. In the end, it is our resistance to the lessons that cause us pain. Chances are, most parents teach us many things that we are glad to embrace, and a few things we want to leave behind. When you think about it from that perspective, they are exactly like most everything else in life. Take what you want and leave the rest. Take what supports, and let go of the need to make the relationship something that it's not.

What about a family that continues to be nonsupporting and detrimental even into adulthood? Wish them well and move on. It is only our attachment to them, and what we think they should be, that continues to cause pain. Understand that I am not advocating isolation here. We need people, and we need people who will remain with us in a close family type relationship, but it does not need to be our birth family. We are only dependent upon our original family if we think we are. Don't forget, it is done unto us as we believe. Just remember that what you say about them, even in their absence, defines you, and not them. If you choose to find a family that supports you and loves you as you are, that doesn't make your old family wrong, it just makes your new family better for you.

If you have a good relationship with your birth family—good for you! You have been able to coexist with a group of people who will be part of your life forever. You have the gift of knowing that although this group of people knew you when you were young and dependent, they are now willing to allow you to grow up and be the you that you came here to be. The lessons found in that kind of reflection are enormous.

PARTNER RELATIONSHIPS

The next big arena of relationship is with our partners. I like redefining this relationship in a way that is different from spouse, or significant other, or even as a soul mate, because there are so many misconceptions about those roles (not to mention a lot of emotional baggage). A partner can be for any number of years. Some will last a lifetime, others for a short period, and still others, somewhere in between. I think it is an error to believe that the length of time the relationship lasts is any indication of its quality. The primary value of any relationship is what it teaches us about ourselves and our place in the universe.

So where does love fit in? From a romantic perspective, love appears to be the glue that brings us together with those we call our partners. From a cosmic perspective, love also seems to be a glue of creativity and creation. In the end, love may be simply our desire to see Wholeness reflected in the eyes of another.

What actually brings us together with others is consciousness. Consciousness is defined as the sum total of all that I am—Spirit, body, conscious, and unconscious. This serves as a sort of magnet to everyone and everything in my life. As you will recall, if our life is a reflection of our thoughts, our primary relationship or absence thereof, is also a reflection of us. This is much easier to take (and believe) if you happen to like the one you're with! Obviously, if you struggle with the single life, or are in a relationship that isn't working, you will resist this idea. In other words, your joy or unhappiness, as a couple or single, is merely a reflection of what you believe.

However, even those of us in a happy, committed partnership find ourselves having to deal with the primary reason behind them—which is growth and evolution. Sure, there are times when things seem to coast and everything is fun and loving. Then something happens, a circumstance, or a mood, or a new desire for one of us, and everything changes. How we deal with it, what we do, and who we become through the process is seldom easy or smooth. Frankly, sometimes it is the hardest and most painful kind of work to do.

Releasing our partner relationships from our expectations is a big step. Just as with families of origin, we tend to build up these models of perfection in our mind and when the real world seldom matches up, we go nuts. Instead of seeing our partners as people put on this planet to satisfy our every need and want, we might start seeing them as people who are walking with us as we learn who we are. They are there to help us and we are there to help them. It is a mutually beneficial relationship. Just as with families, sometimes the greatest lesson they teach us is when something is not working, and it is time to move on.

I met Thom over 25 years ago and although my marriage is probably one of the best I have ever had the privilege to witness, there have still been challenges. I'm sure he would say the same. I used to believe that the reason we were together was because I had asked the Universe for a partner like him. After several years of discovering what kind of relationships didn't work, I decided I was ready to settle down and be with someone whom I loved, and who loved me. Like the good goal setter I was, I made my list and waited for him to show up. He did, and it seemed like a miracle.

Funny thing though, a few of those listed items turned out to be some of the hardest things to live with. I wanted someone strong and smart, and someone who enjoyed communication and adventure. All of those qualities, while ones I admire, continually cause friction in our relationship. Yet, because I was aware of my attraction to those traits, I instinctively knew that if I couldn't make it with him, I couldn't make it with anyone.

One of the best aspects of our relationship is our mutual respect, appreciation, and admiration for each other as individual and distinct people. Although we share many of the same ways of thinking and processing, and many of the same values, we are not the same person and have different talents and qualities. We decided early on that we would stay together as long as our relationship was one of continuing love, friendship, and growth. Thom remains my best friend and there is no other person on the planet that I would rather be with at any given time. However, that doesn't mean that we don't both enjoy other friends and having different experiences.

The most important thing Thom offers me in our partnership is encouragement to become the Kathy that I was meant to be. Often, the times I learn most about myself is when Thom is doing exactly opposite of what I want. (It is probably the same for him.) Yet, our commitment to our relationship, and each other's growth, allows us to work through the discomfort, and find a place where we both can stand.

In addition, we have been extremely fortunate that our spirituality has grown at a similar rate. While it certainly makes things fun (we have amazing conversations!), it isn't essential. I have witnessed hundreds of people who are in relationships where only one is involved in a spiritual practice, and there is still tremendous growth. However, sometimes the growth will signal a time to move on for one person. Should that happen, it is probably another indication of a necessary step on the path.

Which leads us to breakups and divorce. While I certainly don't suggest that people stay in relationships that are abusive, or those that hold them back, before leaving, a person should ask themselves if they are like the man in the story at the beginning of this chapter. Far too often people leave one relationship and turn around and find themselves in exactly the same type again. The faces and names may change, but the actions remain the same. If you tend to repeat the same type of patterns over and over, then perhaps it is time to admit, "What you think about, you bring about." You will recreate the same in a new relationship until you are willing and able to heal what needs your attention in the one you have.

That reminds me of Peter. Peter was determined to meet the perfect woman so he made a list of all the qualities he felt were essential. Then he set out to meet as many women as he could and win the perfect one in marriage.

He met woman after woman and none of them matched all the qualities on his list. Oh, some of them were amazing woman with many of the talents and attributes he admired, but he was determined to find the perfect woman, so he passed them by.

Finally he found her. A perfect woman who contained every single quality he admired. Unfortunately she had her own list of qualities for the perfect man, and he didn't match up!

One final thing needs to be said about partner relationships, and that is that sometimes the greatest lesson is discovering that we don't need them to be a whole and loving individual. Learning to rely on ourselves, to love ourselves, and to joyously give ourselves to the world in everything we do, is something we all strive to experience. Who is to say that one avenue is better than another, except us?

FRIENDSHIPS

I think friendships and partnerships are very similar. If we expect our friends to be perfect, and yet never stop to look in the mirror, we are going to spend a lot of time alone. Just like in our families, our personal relationships and our friendships offer us a reflection of our own consciousness.

Want to know what you think about yourself; look at the type of people you hang out with. If you believe that you deserve equal and supportive relationships, then that is the only kind you will tolerate. You won't make others wrong if they can't provide that type of relationship, you'll just move on, and so will they. If you do not have the type of relationships you want, then chances are good that something within you doesn't offer that same quality you seek in others. Just as in the area of our finances, we tend to attract and keep the quality of relationships we feel we deserve. Want something different, then change the reflection.

CHILDREN

One big area of relationship is with our children. Although I am not a mother myself, I was a child once, and I have had the honor of watching several young people grow and develop through friends and family. One thing I know for certain, children offer their parents immense opportunities to grow. Having a person completely dependent upon you for the first portion of her life is both very rewarding and very challenging. However, that is nothing compared to the adventure of facing her growth away from you as a parent, as your child becomes an individual. As with all relationships, the quality of your experience will be determined by the degree that you offer respect and admiration for your child's unique individuality, and hold appreciation for her special process of growth and life.

While we have all obviously seen many bad examples of parenting, we should keep in mind that people do the best they can with the consciousness that they have. However, in the case of parenting we call poor, much of it has to do with our society. When we begin remembering that we are all connected, we may rise to the point where instead of blaming bad parents for not doing their jobs properly, we start by taking some responsibility.

In a culture that continues to promote child bearing when many people having babies do so out of religious guilt and misguided expectations, not to mention the detriments to the planetary population explosion, then we all bear the cost and results such a paradigm delivers. When we turn away and refuse to educate and help guide future generations by not supporting schools, providing childcare, nutrition, or offering basic medical needs to the adults of tomorrow, we each help to create the world we now occupy.

One specific thing I have noticed is that children tend to epitomize whatever a parent fears. I think this is also true as parents of the children of the world. Whatever we fear as a global society, the children will mirror back to us. The most successful way to heal the mirror they represent, to heal the friction of that relationship, is to heal the fear where it originates—in the heart, mind, and consciousness of the person (or the society) where it starts. When we all, as planetary parents, begin to appreciate and honor our youth for their unique individuality and hold appreciation for their process of growth and life, the children of this planet will be gifts of love and possibility.

TIPS FOR HAPPY AND TRANSFORMING RELATIONSHIPS

• See every person as a spiritual teacher. It's true, every person in your life is a spiritual teacher. Imagine if you had been raised knowing that anyone you encountered was here to teach you something about yourself? How would you behave? Chances are you would start recognizing that everyone is on your side. Instead of seeing people as either friends or foes, you'd realize that everyone is a friend because as long as you learn the lesson he is here to teach you, you are doing what you each came here to do. At the same time he would know that you are in his life to teach him something about himself. Wow! That would remove all sorts of other expectations that we normally have in our society. Instead, we would begin to really appreciate each other. Especially people who were doing things we disagreed with, or saying things we didn't like, because those people would be offering us the greatest opportunity to grow.

• Learn to forgive everyone all the time. This is a tricky one because most people usually fall into one of two categories. The people in the first group think that they have nothing to forgive, so the idea of forgiveness doesn't apply. The people in the second group have had something so horrible happen to them that they can't or won't forgive. My experience demonstrates that both categories will benefit greatly by learning to forgive everyone all the time.

Keep in mind that forgiveness is not condoning. What I have grown to understand is that forgiveness is releasing the past and learning to accept what is. That does not mean that you want it to continue, or that you will let something happen that is clearly opposed to your values. What it does mean is that the past is past, whatever happened did happen, and now you can make another choice and create something new.

When we don't forgive, we are demanding that others play by our rules and see life as we do. Unfortunately that is impossible. Trust me, I've tried! When we resist forgiving, we drag an event or circumstance into the present and continue to live in both the pain of the event, and our frustration with not being able to change it. Give it up. Let it go. Know that your future is not determined by your past—unless you refuse to forgive.

Remember, if everyone is your spiritual teacher, then even those who hurt you or disappoint you are teachers too. They have taught you a major lesson in how not to be, and taught you what you no longer will accept in your life. Bless them, let them go, and create a new future without them. Forgiveness is a powerful step in your transformation.

• It is better to be happy than right. In our culture we hate being wrong. Most of the time we see our relationships as a contest with us either winning or losing. There is another way. Instead of thinking that the only choice you have is to win or lose, start believing that being happy is better. A 17th Century Sufi poet is famous for the line, "Out beyond right doing and wrong doing is a field. I will meet you there." That field is one I call happiness. It is not giving in, or compromising, it is raising the bar to the point where the issue and the people are higher than any disagreement. In that space is happiness.

This is a big one in the everyday world. I have a tendency to take things very personally. Part of that comes from not wanting to forgive and let go, and another part comes from wanting to be right. When I can remember that "everyone is on my side" as a spiritual teacher, and that there is a place to go beyond right-doing and wrong-doing, I release myself from any contest. Try it. It works!

• It is always about you. Something Thom and I attempt to do on a regular basis is to remember that whenever we are hurt, angry, or disappointed in another, it is always about us. After all, in any situation like that, each of us is the common denominator. This is not a popular belief, nor easy, but in the end the only person I can change is me, and the only person you can change is you. Whenever we blame another for our unhappiness, justified or not, then we are giving him control over our life and emotions. Is that something we want to do? Instead, we have the option of turning it around and acting from our highest self in any situation. From that perspective, it is always about us.

• Love heals everything. This is a big statement but also true. If we think of love as a God-like Connecting Glue that holds all of Life together and creates out of Itself, it makes sense. Something that I am learning to do more frequently is to go to that place inside myself where I can feel connected to everyone and all life. I call that space Love. Then, if I have trouble or issues with anyone, and I consciously and mentally send him the core of that feeling that I have just touched, something amazing always happens.

Whenever I successfully send him this Love, whenever I forgive him and let him go, to that extent I heal the trouble. Whenever I freely choose to feel love for someone rather than judgment, I am healed. Now, obviously what I am really doing is healing my sense of separation to him and to all Life. I am also, slowly but surely, returning to the knowledge that he is my spiritual teacher. As I do so, the situation miraculously seems to resolve. I know that it is a big claim, but I believe that if you work with it, you too will see the same result.

Most of us have been raised to believe that we would have the best relationships if people just did what we wanted all the time. If our parents had raised us the way we think they should, if our siblings treated us as we believe we deserve, if our friends and significant others just did what we said, everything would be fantastic. Oh, and let's not forget the children;

if they appreciated us and followed all of our rules and requests, life would be good. While that might be a version of someone's dream, it is not reality. Actually, it soon would be a nightmare.

A good man died and found himself in a heavenly-like place. He was surrounded with people in white robes, who carried huge platters of every type of delectable food imaginable. Because he was hungry, he asked to be fed.

"All you have to do to receive any type of food is just desire it," said the attendant.

Fantastic! However, after he had eaten as much as he could hold, he realized he was lonely. "I want some companionship," he said to his attendant. Once again he was told that all he had to do was desire it. Imagining a beautiful woman, who was completely agreeable to his every need, she instantly appeared. For a while he was happy and satisfied.

However, it wasn't long before he was feeling bored again. Each time he merely imagined people and things just the way he wanted them. The pleasure in that lasted for some time until he went looking for his attendant with a complaint.

"This isn't what I expected at all," the man said with a frown. "Here I have everything I could want and people who will do whatever I ask. I thought the only place you'd be bored, unhappy and dissatisfied was in hell."

"Where do you think you are?" asked the attendant.

Chapter Six

TAKE CARE OF YOUR SPACE SUIT BECAUSE IT'S HARD TO BE SPIRITUAL IF YOU SPRING A LEAK

The teapots used in China provide a valuable lesson. In some households within this ancient region, a teapot is a precious and central part of each family. When purchased, they are treated with reverence, and the best of them are passed down from generation to generation.

It is also widely known that after you have made a particular type of tea in a teapot for many decades, it is no longer necessary to use tea leaves within the pot of boiling water. After a time, the teapot absorbs so much of the essence of tea that merely placing hot water within it will cause it to brew.

Our physical bodies are similar to these teapots. Depending upon our chronological age, we have been brewing tea in us so long that no matter what happens to us, we are sure to produce the same type of outcome by merely pouring in the water. Adding boiling water makes it even more evident. Just as the teapot becomes the essence of the tea used, so too, do our bodies out picture the thoughts, beliefs, and consciousness we hold within it.

If our physical bodies reflect the tea that we hold within, we would be wise to remember two aspects of that idea. First, the physical things that we ingest are brewing a tea that will be absorbed into our physical bodies. In other words, we are what we absorb, be it food or anything else we allow into our bodies.

With hundreds of books and magazines already on the subject, I will not suggest what you should or should not be eating. I also acknowledge that some people may be able to raise their consciousness to a level where they can cure any physical illness, and thereby can do and eat anything they want. However, if the rest of us desire to practice spirituality in a practical way, we would be wise to take care of our physical selves to the best of our ability by making conscious choices about what we ingest, and then being accountable for how those choices influence our unique physical form.

Clearly, different people can eat different things and have different results. I am not sure why, but some people seem to be able to eat all sorts of things and have no negative repercussions. I, on the other hand, must watch what I eat in order for my physical body to react in a positive way. Of course, I can still force myself to ingest something, or as we usually do in our society, eat it anyway and then dull the pain with some form of drug in an attempt to counteract the reaction. However, eventually my body insists that I reject that food and clean up my act. Whether I fight this reaction, or whether I work with the reaction, is up to me.

The famous futurist Buckminster Fuller at one time said that he viewed the human body as a "space suit." I believe his description referred to the fact that we are much more than our physical form. While we inhabit our bodies during this lifetime in a very intimate and wholistic way, our Spirit extends beyond them. While our form is finite, our spirit is eternal. Either way, we live in this space suit while we are here, and it is up to us to take care of it.

After all, who ends up in pain and/or inconvenienced when our space suit springs a leak? In the end, if we feel terrible, it is very difficult to act spiritual and happy. With that in mind, our accountability is very high. However, this doesn't mean that every detrimental thing that happens to your body is your fault. Because we have been so indoctrinated with guilt, many people have been led to believe they are negatively responsible for every accident or sickness that occurs. That belief is much too simplistic because Life is more complex and mysterious than what we will ever know and understand. To believe that any physical challenge we face is punishment because of some failing on our part is to fall into the trap of fatalism.

While old religious teachings may have promoted the idea of a punishing God or Universe, I tend to believe in a world where things happen out of the Universe's need to express, experience, and evolve. Sometimes expression or experience includes things that we don't think we want. Sometimes that looks like an accident or illness. However, Spirit has little concern with making sure that the only experiences we have are ones we like or enjoy. God happens, and then grows, evolves, and expresses in new unfolding ways. Illness or accidents are never a mistake, only another way of expressing. The real question is: What do we do when we are there?

Regardless of what has happened, we usually have a powerful influence on the direction our experience will take. Again, it is not a question of good or bad, right or wrong, merely a result from an action or non-action. Classical physics states that for every action, there is an equal and opposite reaction. That is called the law of cause and effect. In the physical world, this law is easy to demonstrate and experience and most of the time in the physical world, once a cause is put into effect, it will likely produce a corresponding result.

On the other hand, there is the area of quantum physics. Quantum physics and chaos theory refer to the more minute invisible world. There, different results occur out of different expectations. Things happen, not in a linear way, but in a way that jumps from one point, to another point, and sometimes back again, unexpectedly. A person who is awake and aware knows that the experiences that happen in her life, the things that occur in her body, can result from either a cause and effect perspective, or a quantum perspective. Both are exactly as they should be.

From either of these perspectives, we are charged with taking care of our space suit, and at the same time recognizing that sometimes other experiences will occur. Let me give you an example of each.

I grew up in a family from the mid-west. What that means, at least in my book, is that I grew up on meat and potatoes. My idea of a good fish dinner was fish sticks from the freezer to the oven, with catsup on the side. When I married Thom I tended to cook and eat the foods of my childhood.

Then, ten years ago I began experiencing intense pain in my stomach and back. Although I ignored it for as long as I was able, the pain forced me to the doctor's office. Eventually, after several days of tests, the doctor told me I had gallbladder disease.

Rather than give you a complete background on the physiology of the incident, the doctor recommended surgery. Considered major, the surgery required deep anesthesia, the re-arrangement of several organs, and an extended recovery time. Not only did the idea of surgery completely turn me off, but Thom and I were also without health insurance. However, because I had been studying New Thought for several years by then, I was ready and willing to believe that healing was possible on other levels besides the physical. My doctor's opinion was just that, and no more. On my way out the door, I asked him if there was any other alternative to surgery, and he said in a sort of joking way, "Well I have heard of some natural cures with orange juice and olive oil, but of course I'd never recommend that."

That was all I needed. Armed with the possibility that there was another way to look at my situation, I began to research and learned that there were several things at work. I discovered how both my consumption habits and my biology had likely contributed. While the changes in both the way I ate, and what I ate, were challenging, they were easy in light of surgery or the pain of a protesting gallbladder.

Armed with both the information I found, the adjustments I made to my lifestyle, and a vigorous amount of prayer work, I never did have surgery or re-experience that form of pain. Although difficult, this event resulted in many positive outcomes for my family and me. It also is a great example of how cause and effect works with our physical bodies.

This incident solidified my belief in the ability of our spirit and body to heal in spite of odds. However, another story offers a different perspective. In 1996, I came down with a persistent sore throat. After a month,

I went to a doctor and discovered a lump on my thyroid gland causing the problem. Cancer required my older sister to have her thyroid completely removed several years earlier, so my immediate reaction was fear. The same doctor my sister had used suggested tests, but I could see in his eyes that he had already diagnosed and labeled me with the same outcome.

I immediately put on the brakes. I went home and began to do as much research as possible about thyroid glands. Over the next several months, I explored a variety of natural approaches, and at the same time, I spent a large amount of time in prayer. Surely if it worked before, I could expect the same result? Unfortunately, nothing seemed to change.

With my gallbladder many of the causes were easily detected, yet my thyroid problem proved more illusive. Without a physical correlation, I doubled my efforts in the spiritual field. I enlisted the help of everyone I knew to add to the power of my prayers. No difference.

In the meantime, I located a thyroid specialist and went to see him. After an in-depth consultation, he offered me an alternative to surgery by recommending a thyroid supplement. Still I resisted. I wanted my healing in the same way as it had occurred with my gallbladder. In a time of meditation, it came to me that I was telling God how and when I wanted to be cured. That is when I surrendered to the process and accepted that a healing is not always a cure.

Just as the doctor said, once I began the supplement, the lump gradually subsided. While the doctor is under the impression the cyst will never go away, and that the supplements are necessary to manage it, I continue to believe that anything is possible. Nevertheless, I learned in the process that not everything has an obvious answer, and not everything can be fixed, especially in a way that we want. I also walked away from the incident with a deeper level of compassion for others experiencing physical challenges. I now know that when the logical explanations fall short, there is probably a quantum answer at work, and that a healing is not always dependent upon finding a solution.

Another great principle to adopt is that of moderation. With moderation a spiritual person can continue to enjoy many of the physical pleasures available, yet recognize that everything consumed and experienced carries an energy and responsibility. In other words, everything has a footprint. Weighing and measuring the consequences to others and ourselves is a sign of a conscious spiritual being.

That leads me to the other area of our physical body that is affected by the tea that we are continually brewing. This area is within Mind. Again, the Mind that I am discussing is not the brain; this Mind holds the sum total of our consciousness. It is continually brewing a tea that cannot help but be reflected in our physical body and world.

Whenever anyone gets sick in our family, I try to remember that there is something more than the physical going on. Of course, we inhabit a physical body, but it is enormously affected by our mental, emotional, and spiritual thoughts. Yet, if you watch television or listen to most people you continually hear them refer to any illness by addressing the exterior cause as though the spiritual does not even exist.

I think we do that because our society is extremely addicted to the material version of reality. We have a habit of believing that everything can be traced to a physical cause. We always focus on finding out about this germ, or that parasite, and what exact circumstance causes any sickness. Yet, if we are at least as much spiritual as we are material, then shouldn't we look to the invisible as much as we look to the physical?

Thom and I recently went to Baja Mexico where a friend of ours owns a house. We stayed over for a long weekend and had a great time. After we returned, Thom came down with a severe case of Montezuma's Revenge. While the first tendency is to look to the trip as a mistake or error, we decided to put the experience in a larger perspective. Thom admitted that he had been working overtime for several months and was experiencing forms of work stress. He had also stopped working out at the gym as regularly, and perhaps wasn't eating as healthily as he could. While he may not have contracted Montezuma if we had stayed home, he was still vulnerable to illness. Instead of fighting and resisting the experience, he decided to take it easy, learn what he could from the incident, and heal.

Interestingly enough, a man named Jerry discovered Thom was ill. After learning we had been to Mexico, Jerry implied that Thom was to blame for getting sick because he should have known better than go to a foreign country. He implied that Thom should "play it safer" next time and stay home, as though illness could be avoided by never leaving the house. Less than a week later, Jerry ate dinner at a popular and expensive restaurant near his home in Newport Beach where he acquired food poisoning and was nearly hospitalized. This is a reminder that it is impossible to play it safe, and perhaps wrong to even try. The wise person sees every experience, including illness, as another opportunity to stretch and grow.

There is another lesson to be learned from our bodies, and that is in the area of aging. While it is popular to believe that aging can be "cured" so that we can stay young forever, part of me believes that is just more of the materialist's propaganda. There is such an obsession with the physical in our culture that I think it is a disservice to our souls to focus on maintaining our youth at the expense of wisdom.

In the Palm Springs, California area where I live, it appears there are more plastic surgeons than there are family physicians. The amount of money, time, and energy spent on looking young is enormous. Many people act as though they want to live forever, but are easily bored and don't know what to do with themselves on a long holiday weekend. Why live forever when few even know why they are here?

If life is really an eternal, interconnected Whole, always evolving and integrating, then aging is merely a new stage of expression. Why fight it or avoid it? Why not approach it with an openhearted and playful attitude of optimism? Perhaps then, no matter what our age, we will live life with happiness, peace, and meaning.

Sometimes it is clear what changes need to be made when our space suit springs a leak. Other times we must merely trust that something good will come from any situation. I've heard it said by several spiritual teachers that, "we don't know enough to be a pessimist." With that in mind, next time you are faced with a physical challenge and someone questions you about it, good or bad; you can use the following story to answer the question.

A farmer captured an enormous, wild, black stallion and brought it home to his family. The entire neighborhood learned of this find, and they all rushed over to wish him well.

"You are so lucky," they all exclaimed.

"Maybe yes, maybe no," was the farmer's only response.

The next day the farmer's only son Josh was out attempting to ride the stallion and fell off and broke his leg. When the townspeople learned of this event, they rushed to his house with their condolences.

"Oh, this is terrible," they cried. "You are very unlucky."

"Maybe yes, maybe no," was the farmer's reply.

A war broke out in the country and the king sent an army through the countryside to collect young men to go off to war. When they rode into the village where the farmer and his son lived, they left the son behind. When the villagers learned of this, they again hurried to the farmer's property.

"If Josh hadn't broken his leg, he would have been required to go to war," they said in unison. "Again you are extremely lucky,"

"Maybe yes, maybe no," was the father's only reply.

The next day the black stallion escaped, ran away, and was never seen again. Of course, the villagers were convinced that the farmer's luck had run out. Can you guess how he answered them?

Chapter Seven

MOTHER EARTH HAS A SOUL TOO

Last summer Thom and I invited friends to stay overnight at our rental cabin in the mountains. We go there during the summer to escape the heat of the desert. On the evening our friends arrived, we asked them to join us on a walk along Lake Hemet. Serving as a reservoir, no swimming is allowed, although there is camping, picnicking, and fishing along its shore. Dotted along the water's edge are clumps of pine trees and manzanita bushes, as well as dramatic granite rock and boulder formations. A maintenance road follows one side of the lake for a mile or two. It is a favorite location for Thom, our cocker spaniel, Chi, and I as we take an evening walk.

Our friend Melissa and her husband Tim expressed apprehension about joining us, but we assured them that the walk was easy and pleasant. We arrived an hour before sunset and watched the trees and rocks cast long shadows across the road and down into the lake. A chorus of birds seemed to follow our footsteps as Chi ran ahead warning off ground squirrels and rabbits. The dark blue of the water contrasted the vivid blue of the sky, while the soft breeze made the walk tranquil.

Melissa broke the silky silence with a question. "Doesn't this seem weird?"

"What do you mean?" Thom asked back in surprise.

"Well," she paused and looked nervously at the large boulders next to the road, "aren't you worried that an ax murderer might jump out from behind those rocks at any minute?"

Thom and I were stunned. That thought had never once crossed our minds. What amazed us was that Melissa was from the city. She could easily make her way around downtown LA without the slightest concern, but here, in nature, she felt vulnerable and out of place.

This was later confirmed when we took Melissa and Tim to a lookout point near town to gaze at the stars. Standing there in the inky silence of the night, with a canopy of a billion stars above us, we stood staring upwards with the back of our heads resting on our shoulders. Melissa stood in amazement and admitted this was only the second time in her 40 years of life that she had witnessed the Milky Way.

These occurrences were a great reminder that many in our culture are completely out of touch with nature. Civilization has succeeded in cutting people off from the world around us, so much so, that by now some of us imagine ourselves to be safer in the middle of a crowded city than out in the country. What happened?

Up until about 100 years ago, most people lived in rural areas. Because we needed to grow our own food, we had an intimate relationship with nature. Once the industrial age began, and large factories started to mass-produce things, we discovered a way to grow and transport food by means that completely separated most of us from the process. Now, as we go to the grocery store to buy vegetables, meat, and other items, there is little connection to their source. We forget the sun, the earth, and the miracle that created our vegetables, and we ignore the plight of the animals that gave their lives for our dinner.

Not only are we extremely separate from our food sources, we are also separate from many other items that we take for granted. Our clothing is now over 50% man made fabrics, and we are as disconnected from what does come from natural sources—like cotton, silk, and leather—as we are with our food. We drive vehicles that require fuel from the earth, yet as far as we can tell we just pump it out in unlimited (although increasingly expensive) ways, from the pump at the service station.

Each American man, woman, and child throws away tons of paper products every year, and we never once stop to remember the trees that were sacrificed for that convenience. We have gardeners mow our lawns and pest control companies kill the bugs. When we want something we go to the mall, the supermarket, or the Internet and can travel the globe in a minute for any product we desire. Yet, we have no idea where the raw material for those items came from, and what it cost our planet to extract them. In some way it is as though we live on a space station out in space and believe everything we desire miraculously appears in our "energy converters" and then anything we throw away disappears without a trace. Not!

Lest we want to point our fingers at third world countries for their contributions to global warming, pollution, and exploding populations, think again. I recently read that each American child uses and consumes the same planetary resources as 100 children in developing countries. It is also estimated that it would take four entire planets to sustain our current planetary population in the style in which Americans are accustomed. All 6.5 billion of us (and growing) can simply not continue to live as Americans. Something has to give.

In some ways, this modern way of thinking is tied to the past. Before the industrial revolution, many of the world's religions were determined to separate us from nature in much the same way. They taught and promoted the idea that the world was either subservient, or it was something evil to be transcended. Several thousands of years of this line of thinking only helps to make the separation of humans from the rest of the planet complete. Traditional religion seems to have won the conflict, but actually, human greed and vanity seem to have come out on top.

Between religions teaching us that the world was a place of carnal knowledge, and commercials lulling us to sleep making us believe that everything in the world exists for our pleasure and convenience, we have forgotten something very important. If our planet does not maintain a level of health and vitality, neither will we.

I heard a speaker recently tell a story about her home life. This speaker said something that stuck with me. She said in her family they had a saying that went, "If Mama ain't happy, ain't nobody happy." I guess we could say it is time to realize, if Mother Earth isn't happy, then we won't be either.

The amazing thing is that indigenous spiritual traditions have always held the belief that everything is alive (the planet included), and now science is proving that belief. Yet, few of us hear the message. We all know that we share the same atoms with everything on the planet, but we get so focused on our sense of separation, that we forget we are continually taking on and sloughing off atoms every single second. In other words, as I sit here typing, microscopic particles from my entire body are dropping all around me, including when I exhale. Those atoms are going out into the space surrounding me and commingling with others. Meanwhile, every thing around me is sloughing off atoms and molecules, and as I touch anything or breathe, they are entering my body. This continual dance of in and out, and back and forth, is an ongoing relationship. Actually, the same atoms that existed at any time, in any person, are at this moment being absorbed by you and me right now. In other words, some of the same atoms that existed at one time in Caesar, Shakespeare, Lucille Ball, or a billion others are right now part of you and me and everything else.

That is why many in science now say everything is "relationship." When they say that, they are acknowledging that nothing occurs in a vacuum. Everything I do has a repercussion and affects things around me. Everything you do has a similar outcome. I am continually affected by the world around me, and at the same time, I affect it in other ways. The question always remains, are we a benefit or a detriment?

Even if we believe in this concept, the practical reality is that it is still difficult to live each day with it clearly in mind. In our country, we have the benefit of having so much stuff at the touch of our fingers that we become hypnotized with the ease of it all. Until several years ago, I never once stopped to consider how much trash I threw out of my house. I used paper plates without a thought, paper towels for the most minor inconvenience, reams of paper for every little typo and so on and so on.

After taking several classes in environmental awareness, I gradually became increasingly sensitive to the "footprint" I leave on this planet. Everything matters—everything. Although as only one person doing my part, it may appear to be small, when I see the amount of glass, paper, and cans that we recycle each week, I am struck at how much I have done to make one little difference. Sure, it takes some time and effort, but doesn't every worthy endeavor?

Ultimately, it comes down to taking care of Kathy. When I was younger, I didn't even think about it. I ate, drank, and smoked (yes, I even smoked!), as though I was bulletproof and would live forever. As I've grown older, matured, and paid attention, I have learned that this space suit needs my care if I am to remain active and healthy far into the future. As my sense of self has grown, so too has my desire to take care of myself on every level.

I think it is the same with Mother Earth. I used to think of her as a separate, useful thing. Now I believe that she is alive and that we are connected in very deep ways. What I do to her, I do ultimately to others and myself. I take care of her as much as I take care of any of my close relationships, because she and I are bound together in this evolutionary cycle.

Many years ago, I heard a motivational speaker who made a strong point of saying that we should watch the information that we allow into our minds. He used a story where he asked us, "Would you let someone walk into your living room and dump a load of garbage on the floor?"

"No! Of course not!" was our unanimous answer.

Yet we do, don't we? We let people dump on us as they criticize our loved ones and us for any number of little things. We also turn on the nightly news and watch scores of inhumane tragedies. We read things, hear things, and talk about things that are scary and cruel. If you think about it, many of us dump tons of garbage into our minds every single day. Finally, some of us wake up and say, "No more."

Again, it is the same with the planet. As we stand by and let others dump trash here, there, and everywhere we are saying to ourselves, I see no value there. Our lack of concern merely reflects our disconnection and a feeling of complete separation from the world around us. If we walk through a beautiful forest with the worry that an ax murderer might be waiting to jump out at us, we see the world and the planet as something scary that needs to be dominated. Until we see the whole world as our backyard, we won't bother to take care of her.

There is another issue at work here, and that is going beyond our indoctrination of materialism. The more and more industrialized our country has become, the more mechanical everything seems as well. Science has reduced everything to bits and pieces, until we have gradually begun to see everything as inanimate parts. We think of our car, our computer, and our bodies as machines. If something goes wrong, we just fix it with a new or upgraded part, or trade it in for a new model. We seldom see things as "alive." I don't know about you, but anything that isn't alive, I automatically deem disposable.

Once we see anything as "dead," it carries little value. The trees around my house become worthless unless I discover a way they can serve me. And bugs, think about bugs! Even though we see them move, it is clear that they have no value and are actually a nuisance. Who needs them? If I view nature as a machine and effectively "dead," then my body, my consciousness, and the world I live in is the same.

If you want proof for this line of thinking, look at the large number of teenagers in our country who have committed suicide or murder in their schools. They clearly demonstrate that the value of their life and the lives of others around them is unimportant. If we are raised to believe that we are merely machines to be used and exploited, Life loses value and we will see increasing numbers who act accordingly.

Another thing I have learned, as my consciousness gradually expands in a greater environmental awareness, is that you can't "guilt" others (or yourself) into taking care of our planet. In the same way, you can't guilt others into quitting smoking or eating right. Until a person has a change of heart and consciousness, any obligatory changes they make are only band-aids to the situation. If we are ever to turn things around and begin to honor the planet and regard her as a living co-partner during our time and experience here, then we have to change the way we think about everything.

So what do we do? What is a practical way to live knowing and believing that Mother Earth has a soul too? I think the best way is to wake up and remember what a great and glorious gift it is to be alive every single day. When we continually remember, with gratitude, the amazing wonder of our life, we begin to honor and make everything sacred.

Now don't let the word sacred scare you away. If it brings up old religious baggage, you are thinking about it from an old interpretation that made some things special and other things not. A new way to think of sacred is anything and everything that you recognize as special, as well as anything that holds your attention and reminds you of your deep connection to the Mystery. With this new meaning, everything is sacred as long as we see and acknowledge its underlying connection and value.

If we lived our life as though everything were sacred and special, we would automatically do the right thing all the time. We would use only those things we need; we would make every effort to give back more than we took, and we would honor everything for the gift that it offers. Just to offer a few suggestions we could:

- Recycle everything possible, and help others do it as well.

- Support legislation that requires that all transport vehicles, cars, trucks, trains, and planes develop the technology so that they produce no negative emissions. Humans are amazingly creative and could develop these technologies with the right motivation.

- Vote and support men and women in the political arena who are clearly advocates for a sustainable Earth. Work to replace those in leadership who promote the old model.

- Ask that businesses operate in a way that registers their actual cost to do business by calculating their expenses in terms of human and environmental consumption. Then we should begin to rate companies not just on their bottom line, but also on their sustainability. Support only companies that do this.

• Remember that everything has a cost, be it spiritual, mental, or physical. If money remains our primary motivation, we will continue to ignore the cost of human rights, and our environment. Few people say that money is the most important thing in their life, so isn't it time to stop living that way?

It has been said that the only problem any of us really has is a problem of separation. When I remember I exist within a benevolent Universe, I live that way. I have heard there are two types of atheists. Some admit they don't believe in God. Others, more prevalent than we realize, say they believe in God, but don't act that way.

While I have a close attachment to sunlight and bright days, part of me loves the night. When I was young, I would go outside very late and never felt fear. It was as though the dark, starlit sky held me close and I could feel the arms of the mother holding me, carefully nurturing me, singing her lullaby. Perhaps it is now time for me, and all of us, to sing a lullaby for Mother Earth.

Chapter Eight

PRACTICAL SPIRITUAL PRACTICES THAT CAN BE USED ANYWHERE, ANYTIME, BY ANYONE

Several years ago, Thom and I saw a short theater production that demonstrated how change and growth happens for most of humanity. It went something like this:

On a day just like any other, you walk down the street and suddenly fall into a deep hole. "Ouch!" The drop hurts, and you object intensely. You curse and shout for a while, maybe even whine a bit, but eventually you find a way to crawl out of the hole. As you finish your walk, you complain loudly about the poor condition of the streets in your city.

The next day you walk down the same street and before you realize what has happened, you again fall in the same hole. You are furious that such a thing dared to happen to you again. This time you scream and shout at the top of your lungs but no one seems to care or notice. That makes you even angrier. "How could this happen?" you cry and moan. "In this country, in my life! It's just not fair!" While you get some momentary relief from all your self-pity, you eventually realize that you are once again going to have to drag yourself out of the hole or you will never get out. You climb out and go on your way, but you stop and tell everyone the horrible experience you endured. When you get home, you write letters to every city official you can think of about the problem, and call all your friends for sympathy. You are so worked up that you can't get to sleep that night.

The next morning you again find yourself on the same road walking in the same direction. This time you actually see the hole before you get there, but in your resistance and frustration at the unfairness of it all, you get close to the side and fall in again. Now you are really mad—especially at yourself. You mutter and curse, calling yourself every sort of name in the book. "How could I be so stupid?" you question. However, after growing tired of your own complaining, you recall that the only way you got out yesterday was by climbing, so out you go. This time as you continue your journey you belittle yourself with every step. Other people, in agreement, avoid you.

The following day you walk down the road and there is the hole again. This time you approach cautiously. "Wait a minute, I'm smarter than this," you tell yourself as you come nearer to the edge. "What is it about this silly hole that attracts me so?" As you ask, you realize in your fascination that you are standing on the edge. In you go again. This time though, you don't waste any time beating yourself up or blaming others. With a sheepish grin, you crawl out of the hole, and continue on your walk.

The day after that, you walk down the same street and you see the hole very clearly. You remember everything you have gone through in the preceding days, and although you are still very fascinated by something about that hole, you steer clear from the rim and walk on by without falling in. "Yippee! I don't have to do that anymore!" you say to yourself triumphantly.

The final day, you wake up and start out on your daily walk. You begin to head down your usual road, and then for some reason or another, you decide to travel in a completely new direction. You never go down that street, or fall in the hole again.

Change seldom comes easily. Even when we know better, we often continue to do things that have consequences we do not like. I'm no different. It is always easier to think, talk, and write about transformative ideas than it is to live them. Yet, if we continue to fall in the same hole day after day, but hold the awareness and desire to change, gradually we find ourselves doing what it takes to be different.

Of course, we must resist the almost universal tendency we all have in our culture for the fast-food solution to anything. Alternatively, as my friend Jamie says, "add water and stir." In a country where even the most disastrous circumstance can be solved during a 30 minute TV sitcom, we have developed a lack of patience that is extraordinary. We like to microwave our food, medicate ourselves at the slightest hint of any discomfort, shop online so we don't have to go anywhere, and now email, so we don't actually have to talk to one another. Is it any wonder that we reject any new idea that doesn't instantly prove itself in our eyes?

Another tendency is our natural resistance to anything unfamiliar. Our brains seem hardwired so that we seek out any solution that already fits with what we believe. Anything new appears suspect. If you haven't exposed yourself to any new ideas, new people or concepts lately, chances are your thought process is set up like concrete. It will take a jackhammer for anything novel to make an impression.

As it happens, nature often provides such an experience. Anytime you find yourself in a situation you didn't see coming, then chances are your mind was petrified in a particular belief pattern. Ever hear of a man whose wife left him without warning? What about the type A personality that has a heart attack at age 40? Sometimes these life-changing events are our first wakeup call, other times they are reminders to stay awake and pay attention. Remember, Life is about change and growth. Unfortunately, the inclination to grow often battles with our tendency to resist anything new and to maintain comfort. One side of us wants to be safe and secure, the other side to constantly push forward. Until we are able to arrive at a place where these urges can coexist, chances are we will live frustrated and unhappy lives.

One way to balance the two is to remember some of the ideas discussed in this book. To remember our spiritual nature, in spite of the many contrary impressions to the opposite, is essential. Then the next step is to incorporate those ideas into our everyday life. Remember Gandhi and the sugar. If we don't live what we say we believe, we only reinforce an incongruence that contributes to unhappiness.

Also, remember that while some of these ideas may seem amazingly simple, they are not easy to live. Every day thousands of people hear about these ideas by reading magazines like *Spirituality and Health* and *Body and Soul*, or by watching TV programs like *Oprah*. Nevertheless, hearing and reading are only surface level. To actually put them into practice is the challenge. In addition, avoid thinking that because you can talk about them freely, does not necessarily mean you embody them. As the saying goes, "the proof is in the pudding."

Also, be prepared to never arrive. While not popular, it's true. Unfortunately, traditional religions tend to wave the carrot of a heavenly hereafter, or the nirvana of enlightenment by following the right practice or guru, as a prize destination. Yet, my observation is that even when we achieve a high degree of spiritual awareness in our life, there is always another step beyond. As we raise our consciousness and deepen our practice, Spirit constantly beckons. The Zen masters had a question that says it all: "How many years do you have to practice?" Answer: "Until you die." The process of Spirit is an unending deepening of evolution.

So, what can we do, and how? Looking back over my life, I narrowed down several practices that offered me the greatest stretch. Some are big and some are tiny. It is good to be aware that everyone is different, so different people will be drawn to different exercises. It doesn't matter which you choose, only that you do something.

Find a path and stick with it for a long enough time to see if it answers the tug of your heart. In the last 15 years, I have witnessed hundreds of people merely touch on one idea or another and then move on. Many seem to have replaced a superficial material world for a superficial spiritual world. I don't think it matters which religion or spiritual path we choose, only that we grant it enough time and focus to absorb into our being so we know whether it answers the pull of our soul or not. And yes, I even said religion. I think that all of the major religions, and most of the minor ones, have at their root the unity and wholeness of Spirit. That doesn't necessarily mean that their leaders and teachers are mystics, only that the core essences are sound. If any of us takes the time to study the original teachings, and to touch and attempt to experience the heart of that essence, we will be transformed. What turns some of us off is the dominance and dogma, not to mention the weaknesses and limitations of the teachers. In that case, if one organization doesn't work, find a similar one that does.

Unfortunately, even those who recognize their own spiritual nature often never take the time to develop it. They will read a book about one path, then take a class about another, and a week later be attending a group that does something completely different. While each path may eventually lead to the same place, a person has to stay on one long enough to go deep within. Otherwise why bother?

One reason why this trend is so prevalent could be that many new spiritual traditions stress the idea that each of us is already whole, perfect and complete in the eyes of God. Once people find themselves on this new spiritual path, they may think they have already arrived. After all, we have replaced original sin with the idea that we are originally blessed. We are human "beings" not human "doings" which implies there is nothing we need to do. We already are It.

Certainly, we are already 100% expressions of the Divine. However, most people's lives prove there must be more to the equation. As expressions of the Most High, we obviously can't get more spiritual, but we can certainly behave more spiritually. If we are "making it up," our expression can either be something like cancer, where we grow indiscriminately and ultimately destroy ourselves in the process. Or, we can grow and evolve as healing agents of Light. From what I can tell, all of us need discipline and spiritual training in order to be the Light.

The choice is ours. I don't think God judges us negatively either way. It is all a process of evolution for Spirit. In the end, that which enhances

Life causes Life to continue in its quest for growth and evolution. That which annihilates and constricts growth eventually self-destructs, as an obvious example of what doesn't work.

If we want to contribute to the positive growth and evolution of Spirit, we would do well to find spiritual practices that enhance the Light. They are everywhere, but they do ask something in return. We must go deeper than surface level. We must do more than read a book, lend our support now and then, or offer lip service. We must become the Light.

Pray or meditate regularly. When I first began my spiritual path, I found it almost impossible to meditate. It was difficult to sit still and then even harder to clear my mind. As an alternative, I found the practice of spiritual mind treatment. This form of conscious, self-directed, intention setting appealed to my active and creative mind. Its structure kept my mind quiet and focused, allowing me to grow and expand with every sitting.

However, once developed, over the course of many years, it became too confining. After reading books that suggested that our intention is more important than how we do it, and experimenting with alternative ways to connect, I gradually began to incorporate moments of silence in my contemplation. Presently, this works best for me. Perhaps at sometime in the future it will again evolve in another direction. Always, the process is a fluid one.

It is clear that different people are attracted to different forms of prayer and meditation. We must just resist the temptation to believe that the way it works best for any one of us is the way that everyone else should do it. In the end, if the intention of meditation or prayer is to connect and remember who you are, then it matters little how you get there, only that you do. Buddhism and many eastern traditions promote the idea of emptiness, and while that may appear to be a different outcome, I don't think so. If becoming empty is the state where you become One with the Universe, and you recall that state, then you are accessing the Divine in a very similar way. It's the same mountain; you're just approaching it from a different view.

Prayer and meditation are vital to the practical spiritual life. Our lives are so busy, and there are so many distractions, it is difficult to stay connected to the Source of All Being without it. Of course, with continued practice and focus we can eventually raise our consciousness to a point where we become a walking meditator. In that space, we are mindful and aware in each moment that we are One.

It doesn't matter how long you've been on the path or what your occupation: You are a Spiritual Light right where you are. Let's stop any hierarchal thinking that suggests that one job is more spiritual than another, or that you have to know everything before you can make a difference in this world. Everyone is 100% God In Expression, so everyone is a picture of the Divine right now. If you are a teacher, a waitress, a gardener, a homemaker, a mother, a secretary, a student, or an executive, you are expressing God this moment. How are you doing? Could someone look at the way you go about your life and know God? If people can't, it has nothing to do with your label and everything to do with you.

It is the same with reincarnation. While many people say they believe in it, everyone wants to have been someone famous. If you ask, dozens have been either John the Baptist, or Cleopatra, or George Washington. However, no one claims to have been a slave that built the pyramids, or a young mother who died in childbirth. It is the same in our present day occupations. Everyone wants to be a CEO, a sport's hero, a movie star, or Oprah. Few people seem to strive to be a person who merely, "walks her talk."

I have also noticed that few people do things without recognition. Obviously, our society and families have conditioned us well in this way. We perpetuate the myth of fame and ignore the simple reward of doing the right thing simply because it is the right thing to do. Even though acts of simple kindness and compassion don't make the front page, they are the fuel that adds sweetness to our everyday life. I read one time, that "you can get a lot done in this world, if you don't have to take credit for it." Wouldn't it be great if more of us got that message?

Others like to use the excuse that they don't know enough to actually make a difference in the world. This too is a justification for not expressing the Divine in their lives right now. It may be their fears or their complacency; either way, they are putting off the inevitable. While our actions need not be splashy, they either help to enhance the Light or detract from it. Right now, today, there are dozens of people who will benefit from any message of love and encouragement you can provide. Everything you do matters.

Practice ITS. Several years ago Thom came up with a simple formula that reminded us of a way to co-create consciously with the Universe. He named it ITS. The "I" stands for setting your intentions. What is it you want, what is it you desire, what is it that is important to you? By being clear about that point and then focusing on it, you plant a seed into the Universe that will likely grow and blossom. The next letter, "T" is then to Trust. We don't make things happen, what we do is witness them, nurture them, and co-create those things we are guided to do, to bring them into being. Trust also means that we remember that regardless of the appearance, we know that the power of the Universe is working things out in Its own way. The third letter, is "S" for surrender. Surrender doesn't mean giving up. It means letting God be God, and work things out if, when, and how it is suppose to happen. There is an old song that goes something like, "Anything forced, can't be right." It's true. If you ever find yourself struggling to make something happen, think of ITS. It helps.

Make up your mind to like change and growth. One thing I know for sure is that things change. Always. Yet as a culture, we try to hold on to things and make them safe, secure and ironclad. Even if it seems to work for a while, it is still mainly an illusion. I believe that we can set an intention to create a liking for change and growth. Then when it happens, which it will, we will enjoy the experience rather than fight with it.

While I've always enjoyed talking (ask my parents!), I used to be very frightened to speak in front of groups. As the saying goes, "most people would rather be in the casket than give the eulogy." After Thom and I helped to start a spiritual community in our town, I was required to speak in front of the group practically every week. For months I took an antacid each Sunday morning to keep my stomach settled. Finally, one Sunday I asked myself, "Do I want to continue this forever?" While I was becoming increasingly convinced of the value of the meetings, I obviously did not want to do the wild stomach thing for the rest of my life. I decided immediately that I was going to experience it differently. It is very similar to riding a roller coaster. Some people find them exhilarating; others are scared to death. What is it? A choice.

I decided that whenever I felt that flutter in my stomach, it was excitement rather than fear. I chose to believe that the passion I felt for what I was doing was more important than anything. From that point on, I gradually began to enjoy the process. Now, every time I speak, I remind myself how much fun it is to share ideas and communicate what is going on in my soul.

Just like in the story at the beginning of this chapter about falling in the hole, it may take a little bit of pain and suffering, but we can and will change if we want to do so.

Surround yourself with positive input and eliminate the negative. As I said earlier, if someone walked into your house and dumped garbage in your living room, you would probably throw a fit. Yet continuously, we not only let people dump trash into our minds, we actually pay people to do it. We go to movies and watch TV programs that encourage violence, anger, and hate. We listen to talk radio and music that promotes prejudice and tragedy in the name of entertainment. We numb ourselves with hours of commercials telling us we aren't enough, and that we need to buy something to feel better. When you think about it, the garbage in our living room is so thick that we can't tell if anything new has been dumped.

STOP IT! If possible, stop watching television altogether. Two years ago, I stopped watching all TV news and almost instantly, I felt a palatable change in my consciousness. I also only listen to uplifting music. Choose songs that cheer you up (because if you don't—guess what you are doing to yourself!). Listen to tapes and information that make you think in an optimistic way. In most cases, that will eliminate talk radio. If you like to hear people talking, invest in yourself by investing in an uplifting tape series.

Remember, your consciousness absorbs everything you hear. Don't believe me? Then listen to the words coming out of your mouth. We all tend to repeat what we have heard. People can't understand why they are so depressed, when half of the time it is because they are continually dumping negative information into their minds and then regurgitating it. Instead, listen to positive statements, talks, music, and people, and before you know it, you will be repeating them everywhere you go. Guard your consciousness. After all, if we absorb and become the information that we witness, doesn't it make sense to be very picky about what we let in?

On a regular basis do something physical that exercises your spirit and mind as well as your body. Yoga works wonderfully for this. My personal favorite is walking. When I quit smoking, over 16 years ago, I knew that I needed to replace it with something healthy. I started walking. However, instead of just walking, I began taking a cassette player, and now an MP3 player, and listening to positive and spiritual talks each morning. I start out my day hearing reminders of how great it is to be alive. Not only is my mind being stretched and nourished, but so is my body.

Practice "namaste" with every person you encounter. Namaste is a Hindu greeting that can be translated to say, "The Spirit in me sees, and acknowledges, the Spirit in you." In other words, if you see God in every person you encounter, you will be living and moving as a God being yourself. This one can be difficult, especially if someone is doing something that pushes all your buttons, but it can be extremely powerful.

Be about your business. This is one of Thom's favorite sayings. What this means is, when you are about your own business, you stay focused on your world and intentions, and leave others to experience their own growth in their own way. Several years ago, Thom and I discovered that we were spending a great deal of time trying to help others who simply weren't that interested in being helped. While we thought we had the best of intentions, what we eventually learned was that we were using it as a preoccupation to distract ourselves from our own growth. By fixating on others and their situations, we allow ourselves to ignore the fact that by focusing on them, we never get around to advancing on our own path. If you ever find yourself repeatedly getting caught up in the "drama" of other peoples lives, no matter how interesting or traumatic, then chances are you are in their business, and not your own. Ask yourself, what do I need to be doing in my life that I am choosing to avoid?

Be of service. Be of service. Be of service. When I first got on the spiritual path, I didn't spend much time thinking about service. The truth is, when I got involved in New Thought, it was because I was doing it for me. However, gradually I realized that the more peace and happiness I had, the more I wanted and needed to help others and give it away. In fact, I then began to notice that the more I was willing to serve, the more peace and happiness I had.

I have grown to believe that one of the fastest ways to feel happiness and peace is to serve others. This idea is reinforced nearly every time I encounter an unhappy or depressed person. Pay attention—a depressed person seldom talks about other people, except as a complaint. Unhappy people are invariably focused on their own lives, experiences, and unhappiness. If they are able to shift that attention off themselves and practice service in a way that helps others, you can physically see their consciousness shift.

Albert Schweitzer said, "I don't know what your destiny will be, but one thing I know; the only ones among you who will be truly happy are those who have sought and found how to serve." If you want to be happy and practice your connection to all Life, then find ways to be of service. Do it, not for what you or they get out of it, but by what you become because of it.

Be yourself. This seems to be such an obvious one that people often overlook it. I know I have. Even within the quest for spirituality, I have been tempted to think, speak, and write like others that I admire. However, deep down, I know that I came here, in this body, at this time and place, to be the unique me that only I can be. If I copy another, one of us is redundant. Besides, God never makes clones, only new possibilities.

As the old Yiddish story goes, "When you die and go to Heaven, our Maker is not going to ask, 'Why didn't you discover the cure for such and such? Why didn't you become the Messiah?' The only question we will be asked in that precious moment is 'Why didn't you become you?'"

Be creative. If an attribute of God is creator of all life, and if everything is God, then you and I and everyone are co-creators. If we stop that flow, we are stopping the very spirit within us. Ernest Holmes, the founder of Religious Science believed that nearly all illness and unhappiness was due to the stoppage of this innate urge within us. What do you think? Most of us tend to feel that if we are just doing our job, there is no more creative energy we need to express. To the contrary, while you can certainly express creativity in every endeavor, you can also just routinely carry out actions that require no life or spirit. I think if we ask, we each know the difference. You came here to create something every day. What is it?

Get in touch with your inner guidance. First, you have to acknowledge that there is inner guidance available to you, and then once you do, discover a way to access it regularly. Some people simply call it intuition, others have what they call "guides." Still others use things like astrology, tarot, runes, or a host of other tools to access the guidance of their soul. However, I have noticed that most people want to use this assistance not to help their Spirit grow, but instead, to predict a safe and favorable future. I tend to believe that our guidance is available to help us determine choices in the present that suit our Spirit. I am also pretty convinced that Spirit doesn't really care if we are safe or have lots of money. If our spiritual path is actually to express and evolve, then that will probably mean that we won't always have the easiest, safest, or most financially secure route charted out for us. Think about it. If all our guidance offered us was a sure way to win the lottery and have all our desires materialized, then an intuitive person would win the lottery every week, and everyone who is psychic would be extremely happy. It seems Guidance is here to help remind us of who we are and what our soul desires to explore. Listening to it, trusting it, is a great way to be in harmony with the Universe.

Spend as much money and energy on your personal/spiritual growth as you do on toys or entertainment. In our culture, it is very easy to be sucked into the belief that toys and entertainment are the rewards for a successful life. Turn on any television, or open most magazines, and you will discover all the things you should own that reflect a prosperous and happy life. Even if we don't have the money, we are lured into believing that we deserve all the gadgets of our modern age just for being alive, even if we have to go into debt to get them. The problem with that thinking is that if we buy that concept, we can never buy enough.

In the end, our soul doesn't want stuff. It wants purpose and meaning, which can never be bought. I believe if we all spent the same amount of time and money on our personal and spiritual growth as we do on entertainment, not only would our world be a happier place, but we would also experience the satisfaction and peace we all crave.

Spend as much money and energy on your spiritual growth as you do on your body. This point is similar to the last, but with one difference. Many who get started on the path of growth focus exclusively on their body by buying healthy foods, vitamins, and every kind of herbal supplement ever devised. However, many seem to have forgotten about their inner health and the beauty of their mind and soul. (Think others can't tell—guess again!) While the external world constantly bombards us with commercials telling us what we need to do to stay young, be beautiful, and be fit, unless our souls are being fed and equally expressed, we will never be vibrantly alive.

Just imagine how people would be transformed if they got regular "spirit lifts" rather than face-lifts. What would happen in our world if people dedicated the same amount of time and energy to meditation as they do going to the gym and working out? Next time you spend $50 to buy make-up or even vitamins, consider if you have recently spent the same amount on something that feeds your Spirit. Borrow books from friends, buy self empowerment CDs and cassettes. Both Findhorn Press and IONS (The Institute Of Noetic Sciences), among others, offer a huge selection of items that will keep you growing. Be as much, if not more so, concerned about your inner beauty as your outer beauty.

Get intimate. While it is very popular in some traditional religions to deny the flesh and all worldly pleasures, if everything is God evolving, then physical intimacy is also a way to express Spirit. However, notice I said, "Get intimate." That does not mean just get physical with another and exchange body fluids. It does mean that you find someone you can connect with deeply on a heart and soul level. Then if it leads to a physical connection, great. If it doesn't, that is fine too. Our challenge is to recognize our soul's desire to form deep bonds with others. Let's begin to honor that as an aspect of God just like other types of prayer and meditation.

Remember this is it. In case you dozed off sometime during this book— remember, this is IT. If you've gotten this far in the book, chances are good that you've awakened from the heavy hypnosis within our culture, and know yourself to be much more than a limited physical being. However, even when awake we can frequently doze off and forget that the miracle of Life is happening right here and right now. This is It. The sweetness of Life is only available to us when we stay awake and present in the moment. If we are stuck in the past (be it a good memory or a bad one), we are not living life fully. If we are dreaming about the future, either with fantasies or with worry, we are only partly alive. If you want to experience the magnificence of your existence, stay awake, be here now, and remember this is IT.

Spend time in nature. While I am obviously of the belief that Spirit can be found everywhere, I also acknowledge that spending time in nature, where the energy vibrates with living Spirit, is very important. If we pay attention, everyone is endowed with the ability to sense and feel energy patterns. This is the feeling you get when you go into a certain home or business and something doesn't feel right. When that happens, it is a good idea to leave.

Along the same line of thinking, I have noticed that cities have an energy, and it is usually an energy of excess, excitement, and consumption. If you spend all your time there, no matter how much you meditate, you will constantly be subjected to that environmental force. If you give yourself a break now and then, or seek out places within cities that have an abundance of natural life, you give your soul a much-needed escape from the more frantic energies of the city and humanity. Nature seems to slow us down and bring our personal energy back into entrainment with the seasons. Try it. Lie down on the grass in a park, sit on a boulder, or lean your back against a tree and take a nap.

Do your best to recycle and consume responsibly. While the obvious benefits of this practice are the opportunity to co-create a world that might last as long as you do, it does something else as well. Every time I go out of my way to pick up trash by the side of the road, every time I make the effort to carry that heavy box of cans and bottles to the curb, I am reminding myself of my deep connection to the Earth. In addition, it serves notice to other adults and children that we care about the future.

On the other hand, it is also imperative that we begin to consume in a more responsible way. If a low price becomes more important than what it took to bring it to us, then we are contributing to a business practice that enslaves and corrupts people and other countries. While it is easy to point at corporations as the problem, we contribute as long as we support any business or organization in activities that trample on human rights and/or destroy the environment. What happens on the other side of the planet will eventually happen here. Let's stop it now.

Remember, painful things happen all the time, but suffering is optional. You and I do not have to suffer. While things can happen that I cannot control that sometimes cause me pain, I never have to stay there. It is only when I hold on to the pain or frustration, or when I battle with what is happening, that I suffer. By learning to accept things beyond my control or by changing my perception of the situation, I can eliminate suffering in my life. Of course, this requires practice and discipline. While not easy, it is possible.

Look for the good. This is another one of those obvious suggestions, yet I think it deserves to be remembered. Far too often, we go through life paying attention to what is wrong rather than what is right. Imagine spilling a tiny drop of red wine on your new, white carpet. After that, your eye continually goes to that spot, and you forget about all the rest of the carpet that is new and fresh. Alternatively, put one dot on a black board, and ask what everyone notices? The dot of course! Or what about if ten people tell us something good, and then one person tells us something bad? We normally obsess about that one bad thing. Give it up! Refuse to indulge your mind in the dots. Instead, look at what is working; look for the good.

Practice kindness. Nowhere has the failure of traditional religion been more apparent than in the area of kindness. If we focus on protecting the status quo, or our set of rules and dogma, and put the simple practice of kindness as a secondary action, then we are a long way from living love and compassion. Let's stop pretending otherwise. To the extent that we can put aside our own need for self-protection, our struggle to be right, and our obsession with control—can we reach deep and act like God, instead of just talk about It. The outward expression of this is to be kind.

Get comfortable with paradox. There came a time in my spiritual growth where I realized that right and wrong is not a black and white issue. Judging something good or bad is a human trait, not a cosmic one. While the tendency is to pick a side and then fight to the death to maintain it, I now try to remember that if God is everything, then all shades are just different aspects of the One. It is even possible to remember the minute you think you have the answer, to tell yourself that some aspect of the opposite is also true. Funny thing, once we are willing to start looking, it is easier to see. This keeps us from taking sides and instead allows us to see the Wholeness of everything. Several years ago, I came up with a word I called "circulility." This word continues to remind me that in order to be Whole, I must see the entirety of all that is, and resist either/or thinking.

Remember, there are no mistakes. We like to be right. We like to think we have the answer, and that we are doing the right thing at the right time. There is part of me that wants to believe that every word in this book is perfect, and that you "get" every single point that I am trying to make. I could make myself nuts trying to make everything perfect, but the truth is you will read what you need to read within these pages, just as I can only write who and what I know, to the best of my ability. There are bound to be misperceptions in this and every endeavor we undertake.

However, is it possible that the problem isn't that we make mistakes, but rather how we judge mistakes in the first place? Sure, things happen, and we normally have an opinion about whether we like the result or not. Yet, whatever happens usually happens as a natural result of the causes that preceded it, and/or an act of quantum inspiration.

The only time anything can be viewed as a mistake is when we think we have something to lose if it doesn't occur the way we want. Think about it. If I am worried about how you judge my intelligence or spirituality, then I could see any statement within this book that made you view me in a less than desirable way as a mistake. If you are afraid to lose a bunch of money, your job, or your lover, you will think of any action that appears to cause that to be a "mistake." Mistakes only occur in relationship to a fear. They usually have to do with the fear of some loss, even if that loss is only our sense of safety.

On the other hand, if we embrace all change as an evolutionary process, then nothing we do, even the things that don't have happy consequences, will always serve our growth. There is never any loss unless we think there is. If we remember that we are eternal beings that can never die or be separate from the Divine, we will have the peace within us to live as we are called to live. By that change of perception, we eliminate mistakes and the fear beneath them.

Eat chocolate! Okay, so maybe this one is a bit of a stretch, but when it is all said and done, I think chocolate asks two very important questions. First, how could something so exquisite exist unless the Universe was benevolent? Secondly, how could, and why would, a loving Essence of the Universe create something so wonderful on the earth plane unless we came here to experience and enjoy it?

Chapter Nine

FINDING THE SUPPORT YOU NEED: SPIRITUAL GROUPS AND FRIENDSHIPS

While the importance of a spiritual support system was not mentioned in the last chapter, it is an extremely powerful way to practice our spirituality in a practical way. In fact, I believe it is nearly impossible to walk the spiritual path alone. We need one another.

Although it may seem obvious, this advice appears to contradict many spiritual traditions throughout the ages, especially those from the East. The Buddhist or Zen perspectives traditionally promote the idea of emptiness. If the goal is nirvana, or merely to dissolve into the Oneness of the Universe and eliminate all traces of duality and/or the Self, then individual study and meditation alone might be the answer. Formlessness, or the realm of cessation, is the goal from that perspective.

However, that striving for emptiness is actually promoting only one side of duality. Instead of transcending polarity, many succeed in merely denying it, which results in advocating one aspect of the Whole. What about God's desire to express in the material? Involution is the word that conveys our desire to unify with God. Its opposite—evolution—is the word for God's desire to constantly become something new through form. Wholeness requires both actions.

This either/or choice has been with us for a long time. Religion promoted the spiritual mindset and completely denounced the material. Science and the modern culture did the opposite—if you can't touch it, taste it, buy it, or prove it, it doesn't exist. How do we resolve it? How about an integration of the two? Spirit, or the invisible essence of the Universe, is constantly creating out of Itself into the world of form. This form then, is in the process of remembering, returning, and reuniting into the realm of Spirit. It is an endless cycle of birth and death.

Therefore, while a part of us strives to remember and reunite with the formless One, a self-expressed and actualized person will always have an equal desire to participate and create in the world. Only when we assimilate both aspects of Spirit can we consider ourselves Whole.

This brings us back to the importance of Spiritual Community. If it is necessary for us to participate, express, and create in the world of form as a natural expression of God, then other people come with the territory. Moreover, if the material world is a structure of interconnection and relationship, then that web is an inescapable and essential element in everything we experience.

In a very practical way, that means that we seldom get much accomplished in the world on our own. As the anthropologist and author Margaret Mead said, "Never doubt that a small group of thoughtful, committed citizens can change the world; indeed, it's the only thing that ever has." Jesus is attributed with saying, "Where two or more of us are gathered, there will I be also." I believe he meant what we all know. Whenever we get together with others, we generate an energy field that has more power and effect than anything we can do alone. In the areas of personal and planetary evolution and transformation, it takes a community.

Yet, even if you agree, there are many who are resistant to spiritual communities. In most cases, this is probably a reaction to the abuse some received from their former religion. If you were raised and subjected to a tradition that stressed rules and obligations rather than love, compassion, and joy, then you probably want to throw the baby out with the bath water.

However, while we may be leery of any group whatsoever, we now must realize that there are organizations that promote the freedom and the unconditional acceptance that we have always craved. Our challenge is to stay open to what is good about coming together, rather than allowing our past to keep us separate and alone. Regardless of your former experiences, it is possible to be part of a new type of organization and/or to help to create a new model of spiritual group.

Think of it in the same way as divorce or a broken relationship. While your former marriage or partnership may have been exactly what you needed when you began, it gradually no longer served you. For a variety of reasons, you decide to leave the relationship (or get dumped). Once it is completely over, you have a couple of options. You can stay single forever and refuse to get involved in any new relationship; you can find one very similar to the one you had in the past with all its issues and challenges and do it over again; or you can co-create a new relationship based upon your new maturity, growth, and understanding.

We each have the same options in our spiritual communities. Over eight years ago, Thom and I were the catalyst for creating a new spiritual community. We wanted to create something that reflected the equality and partnership that we had within our marriage. We had both experienced several examples of a model we felt no longer worked for us. In case you are wondering what makes a group or partnership healthy as opposed to unhealthy, here are some attributes we believe are necessary.

QUALITIES OF A HEALTHY COMMUNITY

• Decide what your purpose is, and stick to it. In the beginning, we formed our group more out of what we didn't want than what we did want. Gradually we were able to let that go and connect with a guidance of possibility. As that becomes clearer, and as we are able to communicate it and resonate with it, we are doing the work we are meant to do. Some people call this creating a vision and living by it. Whatever you call it, without a guiding purpose, your group will eventually dissolve.

• A true partnership means everyone is equal. Even though education and commitment might vary, and while you might take turns at different roles, the value and necessity of each individual is both honored and utilized. One way to accomplish this is by eliminating titles and dispersing control. As long as everyone votes and has an opportunity to direct, lead, and get involved, ownership is shared among those present.

• Open and direct communication is a necessity and questions are encouraged. No topic is off limits. There are no sacred cows. Every person is allowed to add input and share ideas and if something doesn't seem right, each person may question the process at any time. Because growth, connection, and greater understanding are a guiding principle, open communication is essential.

• Make money an expression of the organization, never a focus. While it may not be practical for every spiritual organization to eliminate the need for salaries and certain expenses, if they at any time take priority over the Spiritual purpose and intention of the organization, the community will eventually erode or become corrupt.

With our organization, we made the decision from the very beginning to make it all-volunteer so that no salaries would ever be paid to the leadership. In other words, those in leadership would never even be tempted to make any decision for the group based upon money. While most spiritual leaders may deal with the struggle effectively, it remains a constant challenge, and we have all seen examples of where it has been abused terribly.

Also, by keeping finances as merely an effect of the group, no decision was ever made in order to make or keep money. We avoided forming "profit centers," or referring to any aspect of the work we were doing as a "business." We also avoided owning any property in order to concentrate on the spiritual energy field we created, rather than the physical location of our meetings or activities. From the beginning, we have operated in the black and money has never been an issue.

• Realize by its very nature, every organization has boundaries. The question is not whether they exist, but whether they allow you the freedom to be who you truly are within them. Although our group is about as open as any I have ever experienced, I know that there are still areas where we draw the line. Obviously, our lines are too restrictive for some and not restrictive enough for others. That's okay. We aren't trying to be like any other group; otherwise, one of us would be unnecessary.

• Have the freedom to walk away if you need to. While this might seem to be an unusual aspect of an organization, I think many of us from previously abusive groups recognize the difference. If you know a group isn't working for you, and you have made every effort to be involved and facilitate the change, and it still doesn't happen, then you need the freedom to walk away. Staying out of guilt or judgment is not healthy for you or the group.

On the other hand, groups themselves need to let people go and not try to hang on in a vain attempt to make everyone happy. Many times during the last eight years, we have been tempted to accommodate the needs of individuals who seemed to possess desirable qualities. Yet, any time we put the needs of individuals before the needs, intentions, and spiritual purpose of the group, we will ultimately frustrate them and ourselves in the process.

Every organization is like a living, breathing entity that is constantly changing. That means new people will come and others will leave. If we try to block either one, we are resisting the life force. While it is part of our cultural conditioning to want growth and retain every part of it all the time, it is technically impossible. Anticipate and welcome this change and the group will be healthier for it in the end.

• Wholeness is always necessary. What this means to me is that a group can have a very strong purpose to transform the world, but if you never take time to have fun and be silly, you are only expressing one side of yourself. Remember, you suffocate if you only inhale or exhale when you breathe. Breathing takes both actions. If you work a lot on inner transformation, be sure to include activities of social service. If you sponsor loads of classes and intellectual experiences, break it up now and then with a drum circle, music, an outdoor hike, or even a party. Every organization or partnership needs this balance. Plan for them.

• Insist that the group strive to Walk It's Talk. Finally, while it is much easier to let things slide rather than speak up, it is imperative that we all begin to insist that our groups live up to their own principles. It has almost become habit to allow the opposite. Everywhere we are seeing examples in business, religion, and politics where they say and promote one thing, and then end up doing much less. It is time to stop. Let's not be part of any group or organization that doesn't strongly attempt to do their best. If we see otherwise, we must be allowed to speak up in protest. Without the opportunity to voice our concern, and then help make it right, it is time to move on.

DON'T LET THE FORM FOOL YOU

Another thing to keep in mind is that your spiritual support system can take many forms. Each group will have its own personality and the people within it will radiate a joint consciousness that will either work along with yours or not. Just don't give up. Keep looking until you find one that feels right and offers the right combination to suit your growth.

While you may not have been aware of them, such groups have always existed. I learned recently that Benjamin Franklin belonged to such a group he called a Junto (pronounced who-n-toe, which means "together" in

Spanish). This group is said to have recommended books, stores, and friends to each other. Their purpose was to foster self-improvement through discussions on all types of topics including philosophy, morals, and politics. A sincere spirit of inquiry after Truth guided their open and vigorous discussions. They also balanced their activities with social service by helping to build a library, a fire department, and a school. Almost makes you want to go out and start a Junto today, doesn't it?

In Chapter One, I talked about the Institute of Noetic Sciences (IONS), an international organization with close to 50,000 members worldwide. Its focus is consciousness and the human potential at the forefront of research and education. IONS can be found on the Internet (as are most organizations today) and offer education, conferences, and local community centers. Find it at: <www.ions.org>.

Findhorn Foundation, the founder of Findhorn Press, is a community in Scotland. This organization started from the vision of a few people back in 1962, and has grown to include over several hundred full-time residents, as well as up to 14,000 visitors every year. Based upon the values of planetary service, co-creation with nature, and attunement to the divinity within all beings, Findhorn is a working example of putting deep spiritual practices to work in a practical way. Also, Findhorn offers educational opportunities as well as work/study experiences. Look for them at: <www.findhorn.org>.

Association for Global New Thought (AGNT) is a global network of groups, churches and other organizations dedicated to planetary healing through self-realization and spirit-based action. Focused on creating a culture of peace, their service projects include nonviolence, recovery, education, and human rights. AGNT offers education, an annual conference, and other connecting opportunities. For more information go to: <www.agnt.org>.

Open your phone book and chances are you will see any number of churches that approach spirituality in a new and open way. Or, check at your local bookstore and ask about book study groups currently in discussion. Go to your local health food outlet or metaphysical bookstore and pick up flyers for gatherings or discussion groups. The opportunities are endless. Last, if one is not available, start your own group. All it takes is two or more people with the right intention.

WHAT A COMMUNITY OFFERS US AS INDIVIDUALS

I heard in a report on CNN that the richest people in America make a practice of surrounding themselves with supportive people who are encouraging and uplifting to each other. They avoid anyone who drags them down or tries to tell them why they can't do something. These people were not employees, but peers who bonded together selectively. On the other hand, the report said that the average person surrounds herself with people from her past. Unfortunately, those people are predominately unsupportive, sometimes unkind, and resist any kind of change.

Once you get on the spiritual path you may find it necessary to let go of many of the people you used to hang around. While this may seem hard or painful, staying surrounded by people who hold you back or continue to take advantage of you is actually the most detrimental thing you can do to yourself. If you want different experiences in your life, you have to change. If you want to change, you have to think and behave differently. Keep in mind, the definition of insanity is doing and saying the same old thing but expecting different results. Staying around friends or family that do not respect or inspire you is insane.

Obviously, the support and encouragement that spiritual communities supply will be very important, but they do other things as well. They offer a world where you can safely explore parts of yourself that you may have avoided in the past. They usually provide education along with a context to use and practice that knowledge. You can't get that simply reading a book. Lastly, they afford a feedback mechanism by asking you to slowly but surely develop your spirituality beyond your present level. As you take classes and get involved, you are invited to go deeper and deeper into living from your highest self.

While any of us can practice spirituality alone, we can sometimes grow lax or fall off course. If no one around calls us on it, we can even fool ourselves into believing we have arrived. A spiritual community of trustworthy co-travelers can haul us back to shore if we drift out past the waves. It can also challenge us in an environment of safety if, or when, our egos take a turn away from the Light.

In many ways, a spiritual community is like a family. Every person there is our teacher, and often it is the person whom you resist the most, who teaches you the most about yourself. Yet, by coming together for a higher purpose and with higher intentions, we are able to develop a consciousness that is more about wholeness, compassion, and love than about creating a self-serving universe. If we are all One, learning to love the other parts of our Self is both vital and necessary.

WHERE DOES IT LEAD?

An aging Hindu master grew tired of his apprentice complaining all the time, so one morning he sent his student for some salt. When the apprentice returned, the master instructed the unhappy young man to pour a tablespoon of salt in a glass of water and then drink it.

"How does it taste?" the master asked.

"Bitter," spit out the apprentice.

The master chuckled and then asked the young man to take another tablespoon of salt and put it in a lake. The two walked in silence to the nearby lake and once the apprentice threw his tablespoon of salt in the water, the old man said, "Now, drink from the lake."

As the water dripped down the young man's chin, the master asked, "How does it taste?"

"Fresh and delicious," answered the apprentice.

"Did you taste the salt?"

"No" answered the young man.

At this, the master sat beside the serious young man who so reminded him of himself. He said, "The salt represents the circumstances that happen in our lives; experiences that occur over which we have no control, especially with other people." He smiled and looked at the apprentice again. "While the bitterness of the salt may be constant, the container determines the taste. If your life seems unhappy, if things become unbearable, don't attempt to eliminate the salt ... just expand the size of your container. Stop being a glass ... become the lake."

Chapter Ten

SHOWING UP!

A friend named Carrie gave me an example of her challenge to live her spirituality in a practical way. In an airport, on a trip to visit family, she admitted she was nervous about flying and found the entire experience of checking in, waiting, and navigating several airports to be frustrating and tense.

However, as a good spiritual student, Carrie vowed this particular trip would be different. Before even driving to the airport, she set a strong intention that everything would flow smoothly. In addition, she affirmed that every person she encountered would be kind and helpful. Fortified with a positive attitude, Carrie parked her car at the long-term parking at Ontario Airport, and took the shuttle to the terminal.

Standing in the check-in line, she noticed how friendly everyone seemed. The line moved smoothly, and she felt great. When she stood one person away from being at the head of the line, she heard an announcement over the loud speaker. "Attention passengers of Flight 327 to Chicago. There will be a two hour delay for this flight due to a mechanical situation. Thank you for your patience."

A loud groan rose from everyone standing around Carrie. She inwardly felt exactly the same way, but was determined not to experience the delay in a negative fashion. When it was her turn to check in, she greeted the clerk with as much cheer as she could muster, and commented on how difficult it must be to deal with such occurrences on a regular basis. After a few minutes of pleasant chitchat, the clerk happened to ask if Carrie would be interested in an upgrade. Without any prompting on her part, Carrie was automatically upgraded to business class. Not a bad result from staying positive.

Faced with a two hour delay, Carrie headed to the gift shop and bought a book that she had been wanting to read. Impulsively, she also bought a bag of chocolate chip cookies to eat while reading her book. She found a row of chairs in a location that looked out over the runway, got out her book, settled her purse with her cookies at her side, and began to read.

Within minutes, a man came out of nowhere and sat in the seat next to her. He too had a book in his hands, and as she watched him from the corner of her eye, she saw him open his book and begin to read. Seconds later, she heard the sound of paper being torn, and another quick glance caused her to inhale sharply. The man had just ripped open the top of her bag of cookies, and before returning them to the space between their two seats, he pulled out two and began chomping away.

She couldn't take it. Carrie opened her eyes wide, stared at the man with obvious irritation, and loudly cleared her throat. The man looked up from his book with surprise, acknowledged her blank stare, grabbed the bag of cookies sitting between them, and asked, "Oh, would you like one?"

Overcome with indignation at the audacity of the man, she defiantly grabbed two cookies out of the bag without so much as a nod. She returned to her book and attempted to stay with the story. Unfortunately, her mind was filled with all the things she should have vented in retaliation. Can you imagine? He took her cookies and then had the nerve to offer her some?

It continued that way for the next two hours. Every now and then the man would grab a cookie or two out of the bag, and each time he would then offer the bag to her. Refusing to let him get ahead, or to arrogantly eat all her cookies, she kept pace and tried to read her book. Regrettably, she only managed to read about five pages because the voices in her head were louder and more compelling than the story line.

Eventually the man picked up the bag and handed it, top open, to Carrie. There she could see that one cookie remained. Taking the last cookie, she acknowledged his respect with a nod, and returned to her book. Minutes later, the man closed his book, got up, and walked off down the terminal.

It was then that the loud speaker announced that her flight was ready to board. Determined to put the man and his rude actions out of her mind, Carrie gathered her belongings and went to place her book in her purse. Clearly laying next to her glasses and pocketbook was a full bag of unopened chocolate chip cookies. All the cookies she had eaten before had belonged to the friendly man who had sat down beside her. Not only had he freely offered her his cookies, he even gave her his last one.

While it is easy to talk about spiritual ideas and ways that we can put them into practice, unless we feed those ideas and allow them to grow and become real in our lives, nothing changes. It is one thing to say, "We are all One," and quite another to share our cookies. Yet, if we are to live happy lives and be part of a planetary transformation, we must do as Gandhi reportedly said and practiced, "We must be the change we wish to see in the world."

Finding peace and accessing the Essence of Spirit is a worthwhile goal that many in our society have pursued during the last couple of decades. While certainly a beginning, I believe the time is now for us to begin to actively feed the Light that we want to grow in this world. If we keep the message solely for our own peace and happiness, and yet allow activities in our world that are clearly not peaceful or compassionate to continue, we effectively promote something else. Our very silence is a support of the status quo.

One way that I find it especially useful to promote the Light is to think of it as a process of Showing Up. People who merely repeat what they have read and heard seldom have the urge to show up and put those ideas into action. If you want to know if a person is practicing what he preaches, look where he shows up and watch where he puts his energy.

As I said earlier, Thom likes to remind people that we all "vote" with our dollars. In other words, with every dollar we spend, we are promoting a business or an organization and everything it represents. When we spend our money to buy things that make us feel safe, we are telling our consciousness that we live in a world that is scary, and we need to use our resources to protect ourselves. If we use our money to merely indulge ourselves in creature comforts and entertainment, we are telling ourselves that life is a party and then you die. In other words, these are my cookies thank you very much! If we shop at stores that offer deep discounts, and yet ignore it when they buy their merchandise from countries that victimize children or keep its citizens in poverty, we are saying that that poverty is someone else's problem, and what is important is that I get a good deal. If we buy stocks and bonds merely to make money and ignore the company's business practices, we are essentially saying that our bottom line is the only thing that matters. In that respect, we are no different from a greedy and corrupt CEO who "fudges" the books to make himself come out ahead.

On the other hand, if we use our money to support organizations that strive to be of service to our fellow man, we are saying we do too. If we buy from businesses that work towards sustainability, we believe that as well. When we support people and political candidates who stand up for human rights and freedom, as well as compassion and service, we further those ideas also. When we support our spiritual organizations, we acknowledge that the Divine is an important and real part of our lives. The voting we do with our dollars is much more regular and much more powerful than any voting we do on an election day.

However, it isn't just our money. Every single day of our life we are faced with how we will act. Once we are awake and become conscious, we no longer have the luxury of believing that our words, lives, and actions have no bearing. Everything, and I mean everything, matters. Some of those actions have instantly perceivable results, while others are merely a slow drip of water against stone. However, eventually those drips accumulate and cause grooves and gullies, and after a long enough time they become a canyon. What we do, what we say, how we act ... all of it matters.

Of course, the paradox is that God doesn't really need us to save It. Regardless of what we do or don't do, regardless of whether this planet and its inhabitants exist into the future, the Life Force will continue in some form or fashion. In other words, even if human life disappears, Spirit will go on. If that happens, it is possible to imagine that God will express Itself in a completely new and different way. We are the ones who are attached to experiencing life here on Earth, so we are the ones, in continual co-creative fashion, who must do something about it.

Don't forget, there is no final destination. If God is already everything, where could we go? Heaven exists within us, around us, and in this moment. If God is a cycle of inward contemplation and outward expression, then It will continue into eternity, always evolving, always expressing, and always returning to Wholeness.

That Wholeness will carry on as the infinitely diverse expression of trying things out, seeing what works, exploring, playing, and dancing with life. There will never be a time when we all think the same, act the same, or are the same. There will never be only one way to view or describe God, one way to celebrate Spirit, one way to talk about It, and certainly never one way to become It. That in itself would be anti-Life and thereby anti-God. To the extent that we celebrate and honor the numerous ways that God chooses to express, to the extent that we come together in Unity, in spite of our many divergent ways of living, do we actually glorify the One.

So what's next? Are we willing to work together to see what is possible in our next evolutionary leap, or do we end the experiment right here and now? The choice is up to us. If we are to continue on, we must do our best to learn and expand our ideas about ourselves to include everything and everyone. Then once we get it in our heads, we need to get it into our hearts. From there, it needs to manifest itself in our actions. It is more than just walking our talk; it is truly creating a world that works for everyone.

We need to show up every day. Showing up means we put our actions in alignment with our heads. It means we vote consciously with our dollars. It means we treat others, and our planet, as we treat ourselves. It means we align ourselves with other people, organizations, and movements that promote and encourage Wholeness. It means we clean up our home, our neighborhoods, and mother Earth.

Through it all, we stay optimistic. Unhappy people can't and won't save our world. It doesn't help to deny or ignore the difficulty. Sure, it might be tough. What gives us strength is remembering that any difficulty has only the power that we give it. Besides, we only face one problem anyway ... a belief that we are separate from God itself.

Where do we start? We start where we are. Today, we spend as much or more time doing our inner work as we do accumulating, or working, or just passing time. Today, we let our interactions with others come from the highest possible place within us. No matter what occurs, we keep our hearts open and in everything; we practice Love. From here on out, we strive to remember that all we do, we do in partnership. This partnership includes everything and everyone, and most especially, Spirit.

In the end, both our life, and our world, is in our hands.

Every day during his young life, Grandson came to visit Grandfather. In the evening, before dinnertime, young Grandson would sit on Grandfather's lap and Grandfather would ask, "So my young son, what happened in your life today?" Each day, Grandson would describe the events that had touched his life.

One day Grandson approached Grandfather with a scowl and rutted brow.

"Come sit," commanded Grandfather. "Tell me what has happened today."

Rigidly, the child climbed onto the lap and then seemed to melt against the warmth he found there. Looking up into the wrinkled, nut-brown face of his grandfather, his anger dissolved into eyes that pooled with tears.

After a time the boy said, "I went into town today to help mother collect supplies. I like to go, I like to help. I also thought I'd be able to buy something at the store, something I've been wanting for a long time." Grandson swallowed and looked out over the porch before going on.

"I was excited to be in town because I don't go often. There were so many people and so much going on. Then mother took me to the hardware store and sure enough, I found a small pocket knife. It was little, but just what I've been wanting. Mother bought it for me and I was very happy." He stopped then, and laid his head against Grandfather's chest. He did not go on.

After a time, Grandfather lifted his hand and gently stroked the boy's raven hair. "And then what happened?" he asked.

"I went outside to wait for mother as she shopped and play with my new knife. Some boys came down the sidewalk, and when they saw me and my knife, they surrounded me and started saying mean things."

"They called me dirty and stupid and other names I didn't understand. Then, one of them told me I didn't deserve such a fine knife and he pushed me. I fell and dropped my knife. Then, another boy grabbed it and they all ran away."

Suddenly the grandson's body went from soft to rigid again in the arms of his grandfather. "I hate those boys! I hate them all."

Grandfather said nothing for some time as he rocked the boy gently on his lap. He stared out into the countryside, obviously reliving his own past. Then he said, "Let me tell you a story, my grandson. There have been many times in my life when I, too, have felt a great fear and hatred for those who have taken so much, with no sorrow or remorse for what they do. However, at one point, I began to notice that the fear and hate was only hurting me, and did nothing to the others. It is much like taking poison and wishing your enemy would die." Grandfather paused and let his words sink in to Grandson's ears.

"One day, I started to think about it in another way. I imagined that there were two wolves inside of me, one light and one dark. The light wolf is all that is good and he does no harm. He lives in peace with everything around him and never takes offense when no offense was meant. Wherever he goes and whatever he does, his mission is to sow peace and harmony. His goal is to love no matter what."

"But the dark wolf within me is very different. He is full of anger, and the littlest thing will set him into rage. He believes the world to be a lonely and fearful place and so he sees everyone as his enemy. His fear and anger are so great that he cannot think or act with kindness. Every one of his actions is misguided, it changes nothing, and it heals nothing."

Grandfather stroked his grandson's hair once again and gently tilted up his chin and looked into his brown eyes. "Sometimes it is hard to live with these two wolves inside of me, for both of them try to control my spirit."

Then Grandson asked, " Which one wins, Grandfather?"

With a smile Grandfather answered, "The one I feed."